THE FINAL
CURTSEY

The author as a bridesmaid to Princess Elizabeth, November 1947

THE FINAL CURTSEY

*The autobiography of Margaret Rhodes,
first cousin of the Queen and niece of the
late Queen Elizabeth The Queen Mother*

MARGARET RHODES

UMBRIA PRESS

Published by Umbria Press
Calder Walker Associates
2 Umbria Street
London SW15 5DP
Alan Gordon Walker
alangw@copperstream.co.uk

Printed by Bain and Bain,
Glasgow G46 7UQ

ISBN 978 0 9541275 6 5

I would like to dedicate this book to the memories of my much loved aunt, Queen Elizabeth The Queen Mother, as well as to my darling husband Denys.

I would like to thank Tom Corby, the former Press Association Court Correspondent, who convinced me that there was a book in me. His editorial, journalistic and research skills were invaluable, as was his faith in the book from the outset.

I am most grateful to Alan Gordon Walker, the publisher, who has provided me with support and helpful advice and guided me in bringing the book to fruition.

Contents

The Strathmore, Elphinstone and Plunket Family Dynasties

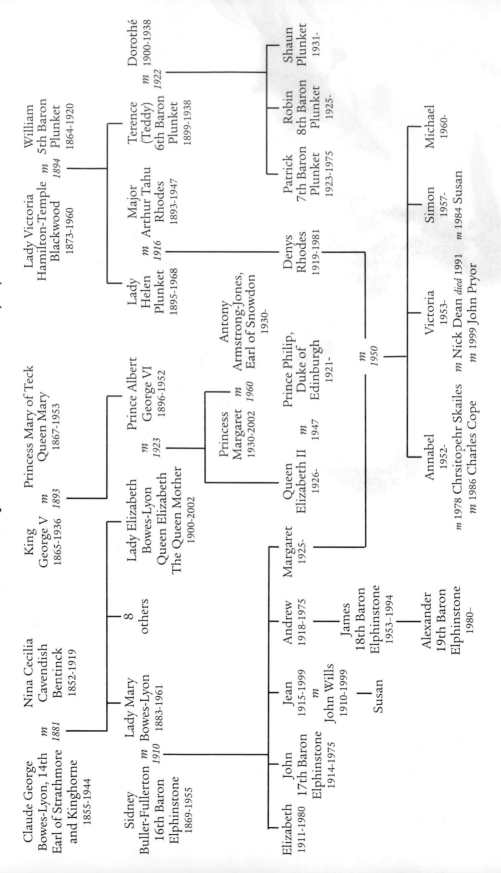

CHAPTER ONE

The Final Curtsey

Saturday 30 March 2002 will be etched in my memory for ever, although it started like any other day at the Garden House, my home in the royal enclave in Windsor Great Park, which had been granted to me by my first cousin, the Queen, twenty-two years earlier. At that time, my husband Denys had become seriously ill and we thought it sensible to move from our isolated house on the edge of Dartmoor. The problem had been finding somewhere suitable and affordable. There was not a great deal of money in hand, and therefore I shall never forget the morning when my prayers were answered. I was out riding with the Queen on the Balmoral estate in Scotland and she suddenly turned in the saddle and said: 'Could you bear to live in suburbia?' It transpired that she was offering us a house in the Great Park at Windsor, the previous occupant of which had been the great horticulturist and landscaper, Sir Eric Savill, the former Director of the Gardens in the Great Park, and architect of the famous Savill and Valley Gardens, which are close by.

Our new home was a short drive from the castle and almost round the corner from Royal Lodge, the weekend retreat of Queen Elizabeth The Queen Mother, who was my mother's youngest sister and my aunt. Royal Lodge had been her country retreat since 1932, after King George V gave it to his second son, then the Duke of York and his Duchess. This house was very special as far as Queen Elizabeth was concerned and she left her mark upon it.

Together with her husband she shaped its grounds and gardens and they spent some of the happiest times of their lives there. Their work was guided by their neighbour Sir Eric Savill. It seemed to me absolutely appropriate that she spent the last weeks of her life there. The present Duke of York and his daughters Princesses Beatrice and Eugenie live in Royal Lodge now.

Queen Elizabeth The Queen Mother had been part of my life for as long as I could remember, and as the years passed she seemed immortal. She had, however, been unwell since Christmas 2001 and I suppose I had been steeling myself for the worst. But back to that March Saturday. It was sunny and bright and the usual chores, like exercising the dog had to be undertaken. Then about 11 o'clock the telephone rang. It was Sir Alistair Aird, my aunt's Private Secretary, warning me that the end seemed close. She had been receiving regular visits from our local doctor, Jonathan Holliday, the Apothecary to the Household at Windsor, and on the morning of her death he was joined by Doctor Richard Thompson, the Physician to the Queen. They concluded that she would not last the day.

I had just returned from a cruise with some friends down the Chilean coast and during that time Princess Margaret had died following a complete breakdown in her health. She had her third stroke on 8 February and developed cardiac problems. A few days before this she had told an old friend that she felt so ill that she longed to join her father, King George VI. My eldest daughter Annabel had telephoned me on board the ship to break that sad news. Queen Elizabeth, although very frail, had bravely insisted on coming down from Sandringham, where she had been staying since Christmas, for her younger daughter's funeral in St George's Chapel, Windsor. After the funeral she returned home to Royal

Lodge, and did not leave it again. I felt so sad about Margaret, but perhaps more for Queen Elizabeth than for anyone else. It is unnatural for a mother to suffer the death of a child, of whatever age, and it compounds the grief. Margaret, the Queen and I had grown up together and when young, Margaret had such great promise, beauty, intelligence and huge charm. It seemed a life unfulfilled in so many ways. In childhood, and when she was growing up, she was very indulged, especially by her father. If she did misbehave she invariably diffused the situation by making everyone laugh, so that the misdemeanour was forgotten, if not forgiven. It was hard to resist her, but she did have the most awful bad luck with men. However the Almighty usually gets the right people to be born first.

I arrived home at the Garden House on 3 March, and found that my aunt was still entertaining visitors. On 5 March she hosted a lawn meet and lunch for the Eton Beagles, and then held her usual house party for the Sandown Park Grand Military race meeting, but she weakened further in the week before Easter, which that year fell on 31 March.

Since 1991 I had been a Woman of the Bedchamber to my aunt, a mix of Lady-in-Waiting and companion, and in her final weeks I went to Royal Lodge every day, usually around 11 or 12, and had lunch with her, the meal being set on a card table in the drawing room. I tried to amuse her with snippets of news that might interest her. It was difficult to get her to eat much. About all she could usually manage was a cup of soup, although her Chef, her Page, and I spent a lot of time trying to think of dishes that might tempt her. But it was wonderful to see her every day, and I would take her little bunches of early daffodils and primroses; any flower that was really sweet smelling. I loved her so much, and I like to think that she regarded me as her third daughter, once paying me the compliment of introducing me as such to a visiting Scandinavian monarch.

The days passed in this fashion until that telephone call. As I arrived at Royal Lodge I saw that the Queen's car was there. I went straight to my aunt's bedroom and found her sitting in her armchair. The Queen was beside her, wearing riding clothes. She had been alerted while riding in the Park; her groom always carrying a radio link to the castle. The nurse from the local surgery and my aunt's Dresser — or Royal Household speak for Ladies' Maid — were also there. My aunt's eyes were shut and thereafter she did not open them or speak another word. The doctors came and went, but the nurse, the Dresser and I stayed throughout. John Ovenden, the Parish Priest of the Chapel of St George's, Windsor, arrived and went straight into Queen Elizabeth's bedroom. He knelt by my aunt's chair, holding her hand and praying quietly. He also recited a Highland lament: 'I am going now into the sleep...' He later told me that he was sure she knew what was happening, because she squeezed his hand. She was 101 – such a very great age. She had arrived in the time of horse-drawn carriages and was leaving it having seen men walking on the moon.

After a while I was persuaded to take a break and went for a walk in the garden. When I came back she had been put to bed. She looked so peaceful. At this point the Queen returned, accompanied by Princess Margaret's children, David Linley and Sarah Chatto. John Ovenden also came back, and we all stood round the bed when he said the prayer: 'Now lettest thou thy servant depart in peace.' We all had tears in our eyes and to this day I cannot hear that being said without wanting to cry. Queen Elizabeth died at 3.15 in the afternoon on 30 March 2002. She just slipped away and her death certificate said that the cause of death was 'extreme old age'. I returned home soon after, thinking that it was strangely significant that she had died on Easter Saturday, the day before the Resurrection. It had been a long and emotionally exhausting day, and I was so touched when David Linley telephoned to say that the Queen would like me to spend the night at the castle.

That evening passed in rather a blur. We had dinner and talked about more or less normal things. We went to bed quite early and next morning we attended communion in the Castle chapel. Later I went to Matins in the Park chapel, and then drove over to Royal Lodge, to make sure all was well with the staff. The Dresser asked me if I would like to see my aunt. She looked lovely and almost younger, death having wiped the lines away. I knelt by her bed and said a prayer for her.

Then I stood up and gave her my final curtsey.

* * *

Later, I was deputed to register my aunt's death at the Windsor Registrar's office. I was shown into the room of a rather fierce-looking lady and we went through the formalities while she ticked the relevant boxes.

At a certain point, she fixed me with a beady eye and asked. 'Right, what was the husband's occupation?'. It seemed a superfluous question; however, after a second's hesitation, I answered, 'King'. I think Queen Elizabeth might have found that almost amusing.

CHAPTER TWO

Upstairs and Downstairs

It seems strange that I once lived in what would turn out to be the last days of a long lost world of seemingly unassailable privilege. Although when it is happening it all seems perfectly normal — especially to a small child as I was. The First World War signalled the threatening clouds and the death throes had done their deed by the end of the Second World War. In the year of my birth — 1925 — the Charleston hit town, and twelve months later the General Strike generated a class war that almost split Britain. The TUC had called out the workers, but the impact did not reach the middle of Scotland. My mother was still receiving the cook every morning to discuss the day's menus. The staff ate in two separate dining rooms, one for the senior members such as the butler, housekeeper, ladies' maid and the head housemaid. If there were visiting valets or ladies' maids, they were included. All the other staff ate together in another room, as in the television series, 'Downton Abbey'. Before the war, in many grand houses, lady guests would be expected to change clothes three times a day, from morning dress to afternoon dress, and finally long evening dress, with decorations and tiaras. The housemaids had to conform as well, wearing some sort of white overall outfit in the mornings, when all the heavy cleaning was done, and black dresses with little white aprons, rather like the uniform once worn by the waitresses in Lyons Corner Houses — they were called 'Nippies' — in the afternoon and evening.

When Queen Mary came to stay with my family, I was given strict instructions by my mother on the required protocol. This entailed kissing her on the cheek, followed by kissing her hand and then curtseying. Of course, I muddled it up, getting it all in the wrong order, finally rising from my obeisance to biff Her Majesty under the chin with the top of my head, as her face lent forward to receive a kiss, which I had forgotten. Luckily this misadventure did not ruffle the calm of the grand old lady. Later in the same year King George II of Greece arrived and I curtseyed deeply to his imposing equerry and shook hands firmly with the King. How was I to know which was which.

There were many other, more light-hearted family occasions, when my aunt, the Duchess of York and her husband, with the two Princesses, visited us. They played some pretty odd and boisterous

Silly games were often played by the grown-ups and enjoyed by spectators, such as 'Are you there Moriarty?' Two people, blindfolded, lie on the ground with rolled-up newspaper batons, trying to hit each other when they answer

games, with distinguished visitors rolling round on the ground being beaten round the head with newspapers which had been folded into batons, playing the game known as 'Are you there, Moriarty?' We three girls were surprised at the curious goings on of the grown ups.

Cocooned in the nursery I, of course, knew nothing about the social convulsions gripping the country, and neither did my first cousin, Princess Elizabeth, who was born a year after me in 1926, that tumultuous strike year, just thirteen days before the mass walk outs started. I learned very much later that her father, then Duke of York, and after the abdication of King Edward VIII, King George VI, was intensely worried about the crisis, and frustrated because his position prevented him from offering any advice, despite his knowledge of industrial affairs and his deep interest in the welfare of working men and women. He was President of the Industrial Welfare Society, and, when asked whether he wanted to take the job on, typically said: 'I'll do it provided there's no damned red carpet about it'.

His personal contribution to breaking down social barriers was through his camps, at which thousands of boys aged between seventeen and nineteen, from widely differing backgrounds, mixed, worked, and played together. He came to be known as 'the Industrial Prince' and, sometimes less kindly by his brothers as 'the Foreman'.

My father, the 16th Baron Elphinstone, was born in 1869. For some odd reason I was rather proud that he had come into the world exactly half way through Queen Victoria's long reign. I love facts that telescope history. For instance my father's sister had a Godmother who was married to one of Napoleon's ADCs, the Comte de Flahaut, who was the illegitimate son of that great

8

My father, the 16th Baron Elphinstone   May, my mother – gardening as usual

survivor of revolutions, Tallyrand, bishop and turncoat aristocrat, who somehow dodged the guillotine and always managed to end up on the winning side. I have quite lately discovered what I think is a fascinating historical fact. When the Queen visited Normandy recently, she was met with cries of 'Vive le Duc', as if she were the living embodiment of the Duke who invaded us in 1066.

My father had been destined for the diplomatic service and was in attendance at the court of the last Tsar of Russia, Nicholas II, in St Petersburg at the turn of the nineteenth century. I have always been fascinated that I had this tiny, tenuous link with Russia before the revolution, and I remember as a child my father telling me about the opulence of the Russian Imperial court, the

Fabergé style brilliance of St Petersburg's high society, and his glimpses of the Imperial family who, despite the formal grandeur of their official position, in private lived very simply, the children being brought up in a very English, austere way, as befitting the great grandchildren of Queen Victoria.

Of course they were all brutally murdered by the Bolsheviks in July 1918, but years later I was told that during their imprisonment they displayed striking courage in the face of the tragedy of their situation, and the letters, diaries and memoirs of those who were in contact with them during the last year and a half of their incarceration unanimously attest to this. The Emperor Nicholas at first hoped that his family would be able to leave Russia for exile in Britain, but his cousin King George V was advised by his ministers that there was strong opposition to this proposal among his people, and the offer of a refuge with their British relatives was withdrawn. The best motives of kings and queens are often constrained by real politick, but George V continued to seek assurances through the British ambassador in St Petersburg concerning the safety of the Imperial family, and always hoped that they would find safety. He was devastated by their cruel deaths, and in his diary wrote: 'May [Queen Mary] and I attended a Service at the Russian Church in Welbeck Street in memory of dear Nicky who I fear was shot last month by the Bolsheviks. We can get no details, it was a foul murder, I was devoted to Nicky, who was the kindest of men, a thorough gentleman, who loved his Country and his people'. A photograph of the Emperor, signed 'Nicky' is displayed on a side table at Sandringham.

In the spring of 1919 the King sent the Royal Navy cruiser

Marlborough to the Crimea to rescue the Romanov survivors. There were only a few, and among them was the Tsar's sister, the Grand Duchess Xenia, who spent forty years in exile in Britain and who Queen Elizabeth liked. I encountered the Grand Duchess in 1940, when she was staying at Craigowan, a house on the Balmoral estate, often used by the Royal Family for short private visits to avoid opening up the castle.

I cannot remember much about her, but indelibly printed in my memory is the image of her severe Lady-in-Waiting, a Russian Orthodox nun called Mother Martha, who wore black robes and black boots. When Princess Elizabeth, Princess Margaret and I were in the vicinity of Craigowan we would break into the Volga boat song, a traditional Russian folk number associated with the peasant barge-haulers on the mighty Volga river. I only hope the Grand Duchess never heard us, because we would surely have been on the receiving end of a rocket if we had been reported to higher authority. We thought that the serenade would remind her of her homeland, but looking back I suppose our behaviour was less than sensitive, bearing in mind her tragic experiences during the revolution. Her son-in-law was Prince Felix Yusupov, one of the murderers of that degenerate mystic Rasputin, who had exerted such an unhealthy influence over the Tsarina.

Somehow, I never really knew why, a career in the diplomatic corridors of power eluded my father. Instead he travelled all over the world, big game hunting and exploring. I suppose his philosophy seemed to be 'have gun, will travel'. He potted grizzly bears in Alaska and Canada and I grew up with a stuffed eight foot high grizzly standing on its hind legs in the hall at Carberry, ten miles south of Edinburgh, one of our two homes in Scotland.

Carberry Towers

I loved every inch of Carberry, but after 1961, when my mother died, my brother John handed it over to the Church of Scotland as a conference centre. They found it too expensive to keep up, and it passed to an organisation called the Friends of Carberry who run it in a more ecumenical fashion. After the family left I never returned because I want to remember it as it was — every stick and stone of it. It had been in the ownership of my family since coming to the Elphinstones through marriage. We also had a smaller house in Surrey, Maryland, my father's wedding gift to my mother, and at one time a London house, which my father had to give up in the Depression of the early 1930s, because, he said, 'something happened to Swedish matches,' which, I suppose was an oblique reference to a failed investment.

He had, however, a fascinating life exploring the most remote and wild regions; the Tian Shan mountains on the Chinese-Russian border, for instance, and he also spent a lot of time in India chasing tigers. When he wasn't doing that he was shooting duck in Egypt, pheasant, partridge and grouse in Scotland and England. How the Animal Liberation Front would have loved him.

He first went to India when he was twenty-five in 1894, and stayed with the Maharajah of Cooch Behar, who had succeeded to his throne at the tender age of ten months. I don't know how he got to know His Royal Highness, but in those days the Indian princes regularly flitted between their states, European capitals and places like the French Riviera. He was a frequent visitor to London and moved around in society and so I suppose they might have met in that way. There were three other big game hunting trips in 1895 and 1896 in the foothills of the Himalayas, Bengal and Assam. I have his game book, in which he precisely recorded for the three visits a bag of thirteen tigers, three leopards, twenty-one rhino, thirty-nine buffalo, ten bison, three python, and many deer, pig, quail and peacock. In 1898 he crossed the Atlantic to shoot duck in the south of Mexico, followed by fishing off the west coast of Florida. His greatest adventure was in 1901. He took the Trans Siberian railway, alighting on the banks of the river Ob near the present modern town of Novosbirsk, The road petered out at Birsk so he took to horseback for the next three hundred miles into the mountains. This ride took twenty days and ended at Kosh Agach, close to the Sino-Russian-Kazakhstan border. My father's companions for this trek were two experienced big game hunters, Philip Vanderbyl and Charles Radcliffe, both army captains.

They hunted in the Kosh Agach area for three weeks, and then headed south for the Tian Shan mountains. Their explorations took them to Zaysan in Kazakhstan and to Yining in China in the Xinjiang province, southwest and deeper into the mountains. They returned to Yining in the autumn and started for home. Their expedition lasted for over six months to regions almost unknown to Europeans. In 1907 my father and the other two men joined the legendary F C Selous, whose real life adventures inspired Rider Haggard to create the fictional Alan Quatermain, in founding the Shikar Club, the big game hunters association. My father then more or less eschewed adventure, but it was another three years before he entered into marriage and family life.

After he settled down, he became Governor of the Bank of Scotland and Captain General of the Royal Company of Archers, the Sovereign's bodyguard north of the border. As Captain General he marched behind the coffin at the funeral of King George V in 1936. There was a strong wind and my father thought the long eagles' feathers in his cap were going to blow away. He lifted his arms to secure them and his braces snapped. He had to walk four and a half miles desperately holding his trousers up with his elbows. That's the kind of story my aunt, Queen Elizabeth, loved. If something could go wrong on a formal occasion, it made her day.

My father gave me little or no advice, but I can remember him telling me that the only things in life to be regretted are the things you don't do. That was a wonderfully powerful incentive to have a go at almost anything, and a piece of wisdom I took to heart. I suppose I inherited his passion for exploration and adventure, and I have certainly had some sticky moments, like being arrested in a coup in Bhutan, of which more later.

My father was regarded by society as a confirmed but exciting and adventurous bachelor. He confounded his family by marrying

My sister Elizabeth, my brother John and sister Jean, with my Granny Lady
Strathmore and Elizabeth Bowes-Lyon, circa 1914/15

just before his fortieth birthday. His bride was the twenty-six year-old Lady Mary Bowes-Lyon, known always as May, who was the eldest daughter of the 14th Earl of Strathmore and Kinghorne, and the eldest sister of Queen Elizabeth. When she was ten-years-old Elizabeth Elphinstone, my eldest sister, was one of the bridesmaids at Queen Elizabeth's wedding in 1923, solemnized at St Margaret's, Westminster, where I was also to be married.

My parents had five children, and I was the youngest, born in 1925. Elizabeth, the eldest was born in 1911; John, the Master of Elphinstone, a Scottish honorific given to the eldest sons of peers whose titles were granted before the 1707 Act of Union, in 1914; Jean in 1915 and Andrew on 11 November 1918, Armistice Day. As a result he had Victor added to his other Christian names. My parents adored each other, and as a teenager I resolved to try and make as happy and loving a marriage as theirs. It is difficult, in old age, to look back dispassionately at one's parents. They were just mother and father and totally distinct from the rest of humanity; far more remote from their children than modern parents. Of course, having nannies and nursery maids on call made a lot of difference, but I cannot remember either parent actually playing any sort of game with me.

My mother seemed far more interested in the garden than in the activities of any of her children. Years later, when I was grown up, I rushed to tell her the earth shattering news that my then boy friend had proposed marriage to me. She said: 'Oh, Darling, really, and what did you say? So sorry Darling, I must go out now and do some work on the rockery'. She had taken little notice and it was not the response that my news deserved.

Unlike her two younger sisters, Rose, who married Commander William Leveson-Gower, who became Earl Granville, and Elizabeth, who both had a highly developed sense of humour and a strong streak of mischief, my mother was in contrast more serious, probably because she was the eldest girl of the Strathmore clan. I have two of her diaries, written when she was in her early twenties before she married in which she regularly recorded going out before breakfast to dig in her garden. Often the rest of the day was spent writing letters, practising her singing, and doing a little drawing and sketching. It was a gentle and rather dull life. The only time I can remember my parents having even the smallest row was when my father asked me, when I was about twelve, to find out what was wrong, because my mother had thrown a copy of *The Times* at him. That was what domestic violence amounted to at Carberry.

I must have been a great surprise to them, born nearly seven years after their last child, when my mother was forty-two and my

Myself as an infant

Clara Knight, first my nanny and
then nanny to the Princesses
Elizabeth and Margaret

father fifty-six. Perhaps they wanted another son, as I remember
being given presents of toy swords, bows and arrows and even a suit
of armour. Dolls were definitely out. I made very efficient missile
launchers by slitting the ends of bamboo canes and inserting stones
in the slit ends. I was a lone child, but not lonely; there is a
difference. Andrew was the nearest to me in age, and I hero-
worshipped him for a long time. He would do exciting things like
making bonfires in winter on the ice of the Carberry pond, to see
how long it took to melt through and he put up with me tagging
along behind him when he was shooting rabbits and pigeons.

My first Nanny was Clara Knight, known as Allah, but not for
any Islamic reason. She was not with me for long. Previously she

17

had been the nursemaid to my aunt, when she was Lady Elizabeth Bowes-Lyon, and after her daughter Princess Elizabeth was born she claimed her back, telling my mother: 'Remember, I had her first'. Allah was succeeded by a lady known as Doddy, whom I can scarcely remember, and at the end of her tenure a nursery governess was installed, the awful Miss Campbell. She was horrid and I hated her. My mother was largely unaware of what went on in the nursery, and as a small child it never occurred to me to complain about the petty tyranny of Miss Campbell's regime. One of her less pleasant tricks, when bathing me, was to say: 'Now shut your eyes and open your mouth, and I will give you a lovely surprise.' Night after night, like a gullible trout, I would obey her and she would stuff the cake of soap into my mouth. That just goes to show how unquestionably stupidly obedient I was. But that was the way things were: as long as I appeared clean and tidy for the hour with my parents after tea, no questions were asked. One of my ordeals was being presented spick and span to the guests when my parents gave a luncheon party. My entrance into the dining room was timed for the end of the meal. The babble of conversation would die down, and I would have to march round the long table shaking hands with everyone. I felt as if every eye was upon me. It was virtual cruelty.

Many people now will probably think that allowing your child to be brought up by a nanny is an abdication of maternal responsibility, but I would argue that teaching the early lessons of childhood to reluctant offspring are rarely achieved without pain by the present generation of busy and impatient mothers. I was certainly grateful, as a mother of four, to have a proper working nursery, although my children did manage to pull a few tricks. My younger daughter, Victoria, was particularly adept at fooling nanny. During potty training she once substituted what should have been in the bottom of the pot with small fir cones. Nanny was taken in and she was allowed out to play.

But whatever the ups and downs of life in the nursery, I was from an early age imbued with a sense of history. No Elphinstone or Strathmore can escape that legacy. The first Lord Elphinstone, of the Peerage of Scotland, was killed fighting the English at the battle of Flodden in 1513. King James IV of Scotland was cut down in the thick of the battle, together with the flower of the Scottish nobility. The second Lord Elphinstone was killed in 1547 at the battle of Pinkie Cleugh, which was another disaster for Scottish armies in the long running wars with the English. This battle took place within the grounds of Carberry, and was certainly not an event for Scots to boast about, as 28,000 men commanded by the Earl of Arran were defeated by 14,000 English led by Protector Somerset. The trenches are still visible and the occasional cannon ball is still recovered. I loved that part of the estate and soaked up the history that drenched the area. The fourth Lord was Lord Treasurer of Scotland and died in 1638. A younger Elphinstone son was created Lord Balmerino and beheaded on Tower Hill for having supported Prince Charles Edward's bid to regain the English and Scottish crowns for the House of Stuart in 1745.

On her father's side my mother was descended from the family of King Robert the Bruce, and as legend has it, from Macbeth, who was a much better King of Scots than Shakespeare gave him credit for. Another Strathmore ancestor was Janet, the widow of the 6th Lord Glamis, who was burned alive as a witch on the castle hill of Edinburgh 'in the prime of her years and of singular

Granny Strathmore

Lord and Lady Strathmore,
my grandparents

beauty'. My maternal grandmother, Nina Cecilia Cavendish-Bentinck, was the great granddaughter of the 3rd Duke of Portland, who was twice Prime Minister in the reign of King George III. Had she been a son she would have succeeded as Duke. My grandmother also counted among her forbears King Henry VIII's favourite sister, Mary Tudor, widow of King Louis XII of France, and that ill fated teenage dupe, Lady Jane Grey, 'the nine days Queen', who was beheaded on the orders of Queen Mary — Bloody Mary — the legitimate heir to her brother, King Edward VI.

Carberry was set in unremarkable countryside, but it took at least two hours to walk around the perimeter of the estate, and inside we were in our own little world. In the winter we skated and played ice hockey on the pond, which, in my view didn't quite qualify as a lake. There was also a hill called Mary's Mount, because it was exactly where Mary, Queen of Scots surrendered to the Confederate Lords and began her long trail to the scaffold, via plots and counter plots, at Fotheringay. It was from there too, that Bothwell, her third husband, fled, later dying quite mad in a dank prison cell in a Danish castle. There is a stone monument on top of the hill commemorating Mary's capture.

The house was built around a square fourteenth century keep and had large additions. The front hall was the ground floor of the keep and had a huge fireplace. Off that were the billiard room and the gents' loo. A passage led to the garden hall with a door into the sunken garden. My father had a smoking room nearby, and one flight up was the drawing room, a big L-shaped chamber with three elegant Adam mantelpieces; the north and south libraries and the dining room. Another staircase led to the armoury, the first floor of the original castle. The walls were covered with weapons of every kind and in a tiny anteroom was the supposed entrance to a tunnel used as an escape route in time of danger. As a child I found this rather scary, yet definitely exciting, though I would try to avoid ever entering it alone.

There were ten spare bedrooms for guests; my parents' bedroom and dressing room; a bedroom each for us children, and tucked away, staff bedrooms. The servants had their own upstairs and downstairs regime, as always happened at the big houses of the day. At the top of the pile were the butler and the housekeeper, who was entitled to double deference because her sister was the housekeeper at Buckingham Palace; the cook, and my mother's personal maid. These last three ladies were given the honorific of 'Mrs', regardless of their marital status. If the feminist movement had been in existence then, I do not doubt that they would have a word or two to say about that. Equally I can imagine the formidable ladies concerned rising up in horror if anyone had addressed them as 'Ms'.

In addition there were three housemaids, a footman, a kitchen maid, a scullery maid, a house boy; the 'odd man,' who did the jobs no one else wanted to do, as well as a relic of a bygone age called the 'Still room' maid, who had her own kitchen. She was the last of several generations of such ladies and her job description was something of an enigma. One of her tasks was to make the porridge, which she did in the old fashioned Scots way involving a whole night's brewing. The male members of the family always had porridge for breakfast from wooden bowls, while standing up, an ancient Scottish habit dating back to the times of Clan warfare. She would also make the jam, and bottle the fruit. She was very old when I knew her and always had a drip on the end of her nose. I used to whistle a lot in those days and when she caught me at it she would shriek: 'Whistling maids and cawing hens are fit for neither man nor beast'. The butler, Mr Fox, was at the top of this feudal domestic pyramid and was almost like a family member, being allowed to reprimand us children for any infringement of the rules. He supervised the laying of the dining table, chose the wines; greeted visitors at the front door and served as valet for my father. His first job in the morning was to serve my father with early morning tea, together with small thin buttered slices of white bread. A full Scottish breakfast followed.

There was a large kitchen garden with greenhouses growing peaches, grapes and figs; a bowling alley and an indoor tennis court. In the stable yard there were staff cottages and stalls for a

Me with the family labrador, Glen, at Carberry

Fishing on the Findhorn at Glenmazeran

carthorse and my pony. The carthorse did all the mowing, dragging a large mower behind him. There were fifteen cottages and a Bothy where the unmarried men lived at a safe distance from the housemaids.

I suspect that life behind the green baize door, which separated us from the servants 'downstairs', was rather jolly and probably there were clandestine romances which those of us 'upstairs' did not get to know about. I don't know what the servants were paid, probably not a great deal, but I do recall my mother having to take on a new cook and being astonished when she asked for £50 a year, plus keep.

My parents were both gardening mad, and I remember my mother as being almost permanently in an old Tweed coat tied round the waist with a piece of string and gum boots and bent double over something in the garden. On grand occasions, however, she could look wonderfully glamorous in a dignified way. She was middle aged when I was a child, but from photographs it was obvious to me that she had been a beautiful young woman.

Every year, in August, we migrated to what I regard as the proper Scotland, to Glenmazeran, a shooting lodge in Inverness-shire bought by my father when my brothers were old enough to handle guns. When we were in London the journey north was by train. And I can still conjure up the marvellous sensation of boarding the night express for the far north at smoke filled Kings Cross and waking early in my berth after we had crossed the border, pulling up the window blind and seeing the purple hills and fast running burns, the scrubby birches and the dark pines. Lowering the window I could breathe in great gusts of heather-scented air. Sometimes we travelled by car with two regular stopovers, one at Welbeck Abbey, the home of the Duke of Portland to whom my mother was distantly related. The old Duchess was rather frightening and very deaf. She had an ear trumpet down which one had to shout. I remember being told that in a period of economy she gave up the *Tatler* and travelled by buses round London asking the conductors, whom she confused with chauffeurs, to deposit her at the precise number of her Grosvenor Square address. The other halt was equally ducal, Alnwick Castle, the seat of the Duke of Northumberland who was a family friend.

Glenmazeran was special. I caught my first salmon in the Findhorn river and my first trout in the Mazeran burn. I subsequently became a keen fisherwoman and skilful angler and a stretch of the river is still named after me: Miss Margaret's Pool.

There were eagles galore, and I once saw three sitting in the same birch tree. In those days they were classed as vermin and on a grouse shooting estate had to be controlled. I was allowed to use a 20-bore shotgun belonging to one of my brothers. Out one day walking in a fir wood, something flopped out of a tree. I went bang and to my surprise the 'something' fell to the ground. It was an eagle and I proudly carried my trophy home slung over my shoulders. I was immensely proud of myself and received the plaudits of the family. The downside was to be infested with ticks and lice.

As I grew older I was introduced to stalking. I shot my first stag with a clean shot when I was fifteen and became hooked on the pursuit, only giving up when I was seventy-two. Deer have an incredibly sensitive sense of smell as well as sharp vision. To get near enough to shoot, one often had to crawl flat on one's stomach for hundreds of yards gauging the direction of the wind, and watching for the sentinel hind, ears pricked and eyes scanning every inch of heather. The natural habitat can only support a certain number of deer and once the grass and heather off which they feed is exhausted, they then die a slow and horrible death from starvation, which is why they have to be culled annually. Others have a view about the morality of field sports, and, of course, they are entitled to their opinion. The Glenmazeran terrain was also populated by buzzards, peregrine falcons, badgers and large wild cats, brown furred with long black ringed tails. My sister Elizabeth had a coat made from their skins.

The shooting season was one of the highlights of the Scottish social calendar and in the last few years of my childhood my parents were asked to act as host and hostess for their friend, the fabulously rich American banking, railroad and steel magnate

Gannochy August 1938. My brother John is far left in the back row and I am seated at the front. My father is far right standing, and my mother is seated seond in from the left. His Majesty The King is fourth from the left, standing, and Her Majesty The Queen is seated in the middle of the front row

John 'Jack' Pierpont Morgan Jnr, who each year between 1934 and 1939 rented the Gannochy estate from the Earl and Countess of Dalhousie for the grouse season.

Gannochy was tremendous fun although, regrettably, I was too young to really appreciate it. There was an endless stream of visitors; all my parents' friends included and I can still remember the magnificent breakfasts. The hot plate had an enormous row of dishes: fried, scrambled and poached eggs, bacon, sausages, Finnan haddock or kedgeree, cold ham and grouse. Then there was the shooting lunch, another enormous meal which was eaten sitting out in the heather, with the butler and a footman, kitted out in tweed plus fours to wait on the guests. That was something not even the Royal Family did. A similar scene of aristocratic plenitude was depicted in the film 'Gosford Park', although we never had any murders! Looking back it seems unbelievable that people lived on such a grand scale, although at the time it never seemed remotely grand. The only comparison I can draw with the present day is the lavish life style of so called celebrities, although their junkets are now much less inhibited.

Sometimes I would stay at Glamis, the ancestral home of my maternal grandparents, the Earl and Countess of Strathmore. It is reputed to be the most haunted castle in Scotland and has a turbulent history. Shakespeare set the scene there of King Duncan's murder in Macbeth and King Malcolm was also murdered within its precincts in 1034. There is the wraith known as the Grey Lady, an unhappy Lady Glamis, who my mother told me in all honesty she had seen on the castle's twisting old stone

The Elphinstone family on the steps of Glamis

staircase. She de-manifested herself as she turned a corner and left my mother, who initially thought she was a housemaid, feeling a shiver down her spine. I grew up with the story that there was a hidden room in the Castle, in which some sort of 'monster' had been hidden – a tale told to the heir on his twenty-first birthday – causing him never to smile again! The story was given emphasis when my mother's generation, young and, believing the story, went round placing white towels out of each window – and there always remained one towel-less window. I am reminded of Noel Coward's anthem to the impoverished aristocracy, 'The Stately Homes of England', the lyrics of which speculated about the fate of 'an extremely rowdy nun, who was bricked up in 1491' and meeting the Queen of Scots 'in a hand embroidered shroud'. It helps, of course, to have an over vivid imagination.

My Strathmore grandfather was an old fashioned aristocrat in the best sense, deeply conscious of his heritage, unfailing in the discharge of his responsibilities, kind, courteous, and sporting too, regularly turning out for the Glamis cricket XI. Sometimes he would come down to breakfast practising bowling with a cricket ball along the castle corridors. He did not care much for a smart social life and was determined that his children as they grew up were not swept up into the set led by the then Prince of Wales, however alluring that might seem.

My maternal grandmother was heavenly. She brought her children up without frills and they worshipped her. She had an unstuffy Christian faith and instilled in all her children her strong reliance on the Almighty, together with an equally strong sense of social duty. She was a brilliant amateur pianist and had a gift for gardening and a capacity for making friends. She made life at

Glamis fun. The author of *Peter Pan*, Sir James Barrie, who lived nearby at Kirriemuir, would come to tea, and once on her birthday he was seated next to Princess Margaret, who was about five-years-old. Listening to her child-like attempts at conversation he promised to include some of her utterances in his next play, and would pay her a penny in royalties every time it was performed. A mock contract was drawn up, but the play *The Boy David* was not an overwhelming success despite containing some of Barrie's finest writing.

Princess Margaret, however, received her royalties, delivered in a bag to Buckingham Palace by the author's secretary, Cynthia Asquith. In 1997, when the Princess opened the re-landscaped site of the Peter Pan statue in Kensington Gardens she was presented with a replica bag of pennies, which my sister, Jean, who was in attendance for the occasion took charge of, as Ladies-in-Waiting do on these occasions. It was a blazingly hot day and the elaborate confectionery prepared for the tea party which followed the opening ceremony, due to be served in a marquee, melted before they could be eaten.

I seemed then to live in a very safe world. As a small child I was taught to say my prayers every evening with my mother and we all regularly attended church. On the reverse side of the coin we were prone to cracking disgusting lavatorial jokes, but never, ever those of a sexual nature. The facts of life were a closed subject and I was entirely innocent and genuinely wondered where babies came from. Perhaps we children were cushioned from harsh reality, although I knew poverty and disease were rampant in the slums of Edinburgh which was not so far away. But a good deal of charity work was undertaken by those more fortunate and my mother was pivotal in this, having adopted one of the worst areas in the city called Niddrie. My father also undertook public works: my generation grew up to be obedient, respectful, and also tough.

We were raised to believe that it was positively immoral to stay indoors regardless of the weather. One had to get outside and do something useful: chop wood, make a bonfire, pull out ivy, weed the garden or go for a bracing walk. The children of a nearby family who lolled around all day reading magazines and novels were cited as examples of degeneracy. To this day I feel guilty if I remain inside for any length of time. Good manners were high on the agenda and my brothers were taught to raise their caps to any woman they met, be she Duchess or the under gardener's wife. And Carberry, despite its size and the servants, was a touch Spartan. There was no central heating and the water in the bowl on my washstand in my bedroom would sometimes freeze over in the winter. I never heard my parents swear and I remember my eldest brother being roundly reprimanded for taking the name of his Maker in vain.

My brothers went away to school. John was sent to a prep school at Broadsatairs on the coast of Kent, and tried to run away, boarding a ship as a stowaway. He was luckily caught before he disappeared over the horizon. He eventually went to Eton and Christ Church, Oxford. Andrew went to Eton too and then New College, Oxford. But school, or in fact any form of serious education, was never actually suggested for my sisters or me. I had a French governess called Sita Rivoir, who came from an obscure region called the Vallee Vaudoise where her father was a Protestant pastor. She was very small and deeply religious. I became pretty hot stuff at the Collects and the Epistles and much

Tug of war. Princess Elizabeth at the front, then Princess Margaret and then me

less hot stuff at arithmetic which Mademoiselle had never managed to master herself. I did however of course learn French.

Many are the times I had to stretch my lips to say the word 'belle' so that it did not sound like 'bell'. After about eight years dealing with me, poor Mademoiselle retired to a nunnery where I once visited her. It is etched in my memory because I was made to wear a veil which, needless to say, slipped off lopsidedly. Also my painted nails seemed inappropriate and I spent ages trying to pick the paint off, so that I at least had two white fingernails to hold my knife and fork while we ate and listened to readings from Holy Scripture.

Princess Elizabeth's governess was Marion 'Crawfie' Crawford, who was introduced to the Duke and Duchess of York by another of my aunts, Lady Rose Leveson Gower. She was very nice really, but then she wrote that sugary book about the childhood of

Princess Elizabeth and Princess Margaret, which so upset Queen Elizabeth, who could not even begin to contemplate that anyone should commit such a breach of trust. Looking back over the years it was pretty innocent stuff, but in those days different standards applied. I haven't read it, and I don't think I shall.

Princess Elizabeth and I were really the last generation of girls from families like ours who didn't go to school. I thought school would be ghastly; you'd have to play hockey. I didn't want to play hockey. I did, however, have dancing lessons and I was at the dancing school in Edinburgh the day the abdication of King Edward VIII was announced. To my eternal shame I hopped around the room chanting: 'My uncle Bertie is going to be King'. Very soon afterwards 'Uncle Bertie' became 'Sir'. Princess Elizabeth became Heiress Presumptive, the 'Presumptive' inserted just in case she later had a brother. I believed she hoped she might have one and be let off the hook, but deep down she knew that wasn't very likely. She accepted that she would be Queen one day, but thought it was a long way off. Sadly it came to her much sooner than she expected.

Much has been written and said about the so called bad blood between Queen Elizabeth and the Duke and Duchess of Windsor, but not once in all the years I was with my aunt — not once — did I ever hear her say anything remotely unpleasant about them. Becoming Queen was not what she wanted, or expected, but when it happened she accepted it, calling it 'this intolerable honour' and became the most successful Queen Consort in the history of the British monarchy.

Many years later when the Windsor's house in Paris was restored after the death of the Duchess, a collection of Christmas cards from

Queen Elizabeth was discovered, each of them inscribed affectionately, giving the lie to the popular view that my aunt bore a deep rooted grudge towards the Duke and Duchess for precipitating her husband into sovereignty, and therefore because of the stresses and strains involved, particularly during the war, prematurely ending his life. Strangely these cards and other correspondence were found in the Duke's bath. Apparently, American style, he always used the shower. Tellingly the only card which retained its envelope was from a rather second rank royal who shall be nameless. It was addressed to 'Their Royal Highnesses, the Duke and Duchess of Windsor'. The Duchess, of course, was never granted royal status and was buried at Windsor in a coffin with a brass plate inscribed 'Wallis, Duchess of Windsor'.

My parents would rent a house in London for the summer season when my two sisters would do the debutante rounds of balls and parties. This was known as 'coming out', which doesn't mean what it does today, but being presented to the King and Queen at Court, wearing white dresses with trains, long white gloves and three ostrich feathers on top of the head. Crowds used to gather in the Mall to watch the cars containing the debutantes queuing to drop them off at Buckingham Palace. The presentation involved having your name announced by the Lord Chamberlain and then curtseying in turn to the King and Queen. The names of those participating in this ritual were then entered in an official register and they were then deemed to have a passport to so called high society. The Queen finally brought the curtain down on it all in 1958, the demand for entrée having become unmanageable. As Princess Margaret was said to have remarked: 'We had to end it. Every tart in London was getting in'.

Quite! By the time I was eligible when I was eighteen in 1943, the presentations were in abeyance, for which I was very grateful. It took a world war to save me from such an embarrassing rite of passage, although it was never regarded as such, only as a regular hurdle in the course of growing up.

My memories of Queen Elizabeth started when I was about five with my annual visits to Birkhall, on the Balmoral estate. The house dates from the eighteenth century, and since 1930 it had been lent by King George V to the Duke and Duchess of York to use when the Royal Family migrated to Scotland for their summer and early autumn holiday. When I was very young I told the King and Queen that if I ever married I would love to spend my honeymoon there and when I did get married, to Denys Rhodes, a

Guests at Carberry. The King and Queen and Princess Margaret watch participants in the game 'Are you there Moriarty?'. My mother stands next to her sister, Queen Elizabeth, and in the background can be glimpsed the royal nanny, Clara Knight, known as Allah

cousin of Patrick Plunket, in 1950, they angelically remembered and let us have the house for two weeks, generously installing a cook as well. Three years earlier Princess Elizabeth and Prince Philip spent part of their honeymoon there too. My cousin wrote to me from Birkhall, two weeks after her marriage describing its beauty under the December snows, the peace and quiet and how the local people left them undisturbed. 'Scots are nice that way' she said. There were shooting outings, but the stalkers who because of the eccentricity of their attire resembled a very mixed rag bag, rather took the Princess aback. 'We were', she said, confronted with the most scurvy looking lot of ruffians that I have ever seen!' Thereafter, having found her army boots and leather jerkin 'I looked more in keeping with everyone else'. She added: 'I couldn't help wishing that a photographer would come along, just for once, as he would never have believed what he saw! I imagined that I might be like a female Russian commando leader followed by her faithful cut throats, all armed to the teeth with rifles'.

The seclusion of Birkhall was in strong contrast to the first part of her honeymoon which was spent at Broadlands, the Hampshire home of Earl Mountbatten, where she and Philip had little escape from a curious press and public; the crowds arriving on foot, by car and by motor coach, besieging Romsey Abbey, where they attended morning service on the first Sunday of their week's stay. Those who couldn't get inside climbed on tomb stones, and propped ladders and chairs against the walls so as to peer through the windows. One family, it was reported, even carried their sideboard into the churchyard and stood on it to watch the couple at prayer. Others queued for a chance to sit in the pew occupied a short while earlier by royalty.

The Princess in her letter told me that although she liked Broadlands, 'we were terribly pestered by the Press, and, of course, our going to church at Romsey Abbey was a most vulgar and disgraceful affair'. However she was obviously content with the state of matrimony and in a postscript wrote: 'I'm blissfully happy, in case you weren't aware of the fact and I'm enjoying being married to the best and nicest man in the world'.

Birkhall is a very special place and the greatest fun of the whole year was my annual childhood visit to join Princess Elizabeth and Princess Margaret. The garden descended steeply to the river Muick and sometimes we would picnic on an island in the river. I remember a rather sick making contest to see how many slices of brown bread and golden syrup we could eat. My record was twelve slices and I always won with ease which is not really a matter to be proud of. Princess Elizabeth, just ten months younger than me, was a natural playmate. We endlessly cavorted as horses, which was her idea. We galloped round and round. We were horses of every kind: carthorses, racehorses, and circus horses. We spent a lot of time as circus horses and it was obligatory to neigh. Another game was called 'catching happy days'. This involved catching the leaves falling from the trees. There was a gramophone and just one record, either 'Land of Hope and Glory or 'Jerusalem'. I can't remember which, but we played it all the time. Princess Margaret used to keep me awake at night as I was given the next door bedroom. The walls were very thin and Margaret would sing 'Old Macdonald had a Farm' which goes on and on with its refrain of animal noises. It was an incessant chant and I prayed that she would exhaust herself and fall asleep. We used our imaginations and were easily amused. How we passed our time must seem extraordinarily unreal to the present generation of computer game children, who only seem happy with much more sophisticated pursuits.

In childhood, the only time I can recall Princess Elizabeth pulling rank was when we squabbled over the ownership of a wooden seat outside the front door of Birkhall. Territorially she claimed it declaring: 'I'm the biggest "P" for Princess'. My aunt had somehow acquired the nickname 'Peter' from my eldest sister, Elizabeth. Queen Elizabeth and the King would always come up to the nursery and kiss their children goodnight. The Queen was sheer magic with her children, as she was with the public, particularly during the Second World War air raids, when as a great unifying force, she was described by a patriotic media as 'the Queen of the Blitz'.

I well remember the preparations for the coronation of the King and Queen in 1937. My cousins had specially designed dresses, robes and coronets. Princess Margaret was a couple of months short of eight, but I was not invited as I was thought to be too young. Everybody else seemed to be going, shaking the mothballs from their robes and ermine – probably rabbit in some cases – including my mother and father as a peer and peeress and also my brothers and sisters.

I was particularly put out because a girl I knew of my own age, who had a tiny drop of Royal blood, was attending in a lovely long dress. However on the morning of the great day I was taken to Buckingham Palace, kitted out in my best pink coat with a velvet collar, where I had breakfast with my cousins and was then taken along the corridor to see the King and Queen in their finery. The King was wearing a white shirt, breeches and stockings and a crimson satin coat and the Queen a wonderful be-sequined long dress. Then a Page came in and said it was time for the Princesses to go down to the Grand Entrance where their carriage was waiting. My only other memory of the coronation was looking out of a window of the palace and watching the procession of the Indian maharajahs and princes, their tunics, coats and turbans encrusted with diamonds worth a king's ransom. They looked wonderfully grand and romantic. Even the horses pulling their carriages were clad in the most gorgeous tack and over seventy years on the memory of that fantastic procession remains vivid.

The 1937 coronation was the last enactment of British style pomp and circumstance before Europe was plunged into war. Princess Elizabeth recorded her day in a lined exercise book, neatly tied round with a piece of pink ribbon and with a touching dedication inscribed in red crayon on the cover. It read: 'The Coronation, 12th May 1937, to Mummy and Papa, in memory of their coronation, from Lilibet by Herself. An Account of the Coronation.' It is preserved in the Royal archives at Windsor Castle and its ingenuous freshness has lost nothing by the passing of the years, setting the scene in my view more effectively than the prose of official historians. I got a small mention on the last page.

I did make it to the coronation of Queen Elizabeth II, sixteen years later, as one of the privileged 8000 that had been invited to the Abbey. We all received a list of do's and don'ts from the Earl Marshal, the Duke of Norfolk, the choreographer of the occasion, including notes of what we should wear. I was pregnant with my second daughter, Victoria, but contrived to match up by wearing my wedding dress cunningly let out around the waist. My husband Denys of course came too in the full dress uniform of the Rifle Brigade. Throughout the ceremony we sat on stools stamped with the royal cypher, and were allowed to take them away as souvenirs.

Setting out for the coronation, 1953. I was
pregnant with my second daughter, Victoria

One is now, a touch *lesè majesté* in the loo and the other in my
bedroom. We had to get there hours before the action started and
were rigidly enclosed. At the time I wondered about the predicament
of the more elderly peers and peeresses when nature beset them.

In 1938 and 1939, despite the sabre rattling coming from
Berlin my routine continued. In the last August of the peace I was
dispatched to Birkhall as usual to keep Princess Elizabeth and
Princess Margaret company. The King and Queen must have been
desperately worried, but they never imparted the deepening sense
of crisis to us. I didn't know it, but on 22 August Europe
shuddered at the announcement of the Soviet-German non-
aggression pact and then groaned in anguished apprehension for
few doubted that this could but betoken war. The King and
Queen at once returned to London.

The tide of war seemed inexorable and at dawn on 1

September, the Wehrmacht crossed the Polish frontier. The timing of the ultimatum sent to the German Chancellor, demanding he withdraw his troops or accept a declaration of war by Britain and France, had passed and so we were at war from eleven o'clock on the morning of Sunday 3 September. We three girls were in Craithie Kirk for the morning service at this time. The Minister, a small, spare man called Dr Lamb preached a highly emotional sermon and told his flock that the uneasy peace which had prevailed since the end of the First World War was now over. It seemed unreal, yet in a strange way it was exciting and it was impossible not to dream of adventure and derring-do. We were so utterly ignorant about the actual horrors of war.

Our routine continued. Every evening at six the King and Queen would telephone and speak to their daughters. We had a French governess, Georgina Guerin, who when the war got fully under way, would return to France and become a leading light in the Resistance. There was also one of the Queen's Ladies-in-Waiting, Lettice Bowlby, to keep and eye on us. Our two carers were not best of friends and behind her back Georgina called Lettice 'la sale Bowlbee'. I was just fourteen, Princess Elizabeth thirteen and Princess Margaret was only nine. We were at war but nothing much was happening. There was no sign of Panzer divisions or enemy parachutists. We did lessons of a sort; rode our ponies, went on picnics, all the usual things. Then the week before Christmas the Queen telephoned to say it was safe for the Princesses to go to Sandringham in Norfolk, even though it was close to one of the coast lines where a German invasion was considered most likely. I returned to Carberry for our family Christmas. I tried on my gas mask, just to be on the safe side, and awaited what was to come.

CHAPTER THREE

War time with the Windsors

The war made its impact on our daily lives at Carberry as it did for all families. My two brothers put on khaki and set off to join their regiments, John to the Black Watch and Andrew to the Cameron Highlanders. Occasionally there were air raids: to begin with we trailed down to the front hall, which as the most ancient part of the house had the thickest walls and sat there shivering until the all-clear whined. But soon we gave even that up and remained comfortably tucked up in bed, listening to the thumping of the guns defending the Forth Bridge. Sometimes I was unable to resist the temptation to get dressed and wander solitary in the grounds watching the search lights weaving strange and beautiful patterns in the blackness of the night. Every so often a silver speck would be trapped, as if transfixed on the point of a spear and the guns would then thunder their defiance.

Once I was out seeking to shoot a rabbit or pigeon for the pot with my .22 rifle, when I heard an aeroplane coming; it was flying very low. I could easily see the Swastika on its wings, so I immediately fired my whole magazine of eight bullets at it, in the vain hope that I might just hit the petrol tank. Alas, it flew away unscathed, but I felt better for having made a tiny personal contribution to the war effort.

In those days I almost had Carberry to myself. My father was busy in Edinburgh and my mother had joined the Women's

41

Voluntary Service, now the WRVS. My eldest sister, Elizabeth was a VAD in an Edinburgh hospital and very aware of the presence of God in her life. She came under the spell of an order of Anglican nuns of which she later became a lay member. My next sister, Jean had enjoyed a rather wild coming out season and was a born flirt. Even at the age of eighty she had lost none of her charm and attraction. When she was first grown up my parents allowed her to have a weekend party at our house Maryland only on the condition that she was strictly chaperoned throughout. A lady duly arrived from a wonderful organisation called Universal Aunts. Jean found her presence something of hindrance to her idea of having fun. She solved it by telling the poor woman that all her young male guests, every man of them from the Household Cavalry, had been recalled to barracks and that therefore the weekend was cancelled.

The men drove off for half a mile, only to re-emerge when they safely knew that the chaperone's taxi was out of sight. Jean married one of her clandestine guests and at the beginning of the war was living in Northamptonshire with her two small children. Her husband, John Wills had been posted to the Middle East and was not to return until the war ended. Jean's in-laws, Captain Benjy and Hilda Wills had an estate called Applecross on the north west coast of Scotland. It was a fisherman's dream and the salmon often seemed to be lying in layers in the deeper pools. Jean used to invite me there and one day we took the family's small yacht out to an island which had a row of deserted cottages. We anchored there to picnic and to our astonishment saw smoke rising from one of the cottage chimneys. Then a young kilted man approached, claiming to be a university student who needed complete solitude so as to write his thesis. He seemed perfectly genuine and we swallowed his story, even giving him what was left over from our provisions to help him replenish his scanty supplies. Some time later we discovered that he and an accomplice were Nazi sympathisers reporting on Allied shipping movements. We had unwittingly aided and abetted a couple of enemy spies.

After my brothers had joined their regiments, my father, who was seventy in 1939, had been appointed Chairman of a board which adjudicated on the appeals of conscientious objectors. It was a difficult and unpleasant task, compounded on one distressing occasion by the appearance before him of William Douglas-Home, the son of the 13th Earl of Home, his oldest friend and best man at his wedding. Whatever the verdict, William subsequently became an officer in the Royal Armoured Corps and in 1944 refused on moral grounds to take part in an attack on Le Havre because the thousands of refugees packed into the town had not been evacuated. Over 5000 of them were killed in the operation, but William was sentenced to a year's hard labour, serving eight months for refusing to obey an order. Courage takes different forms. He later became a successful writer and dramatist. His oldest brother, Sir Alex Douglas-Home, was Conservative Prime Minister between 1963 and 1964.

I remember my brother John coming home on embarkation leave looking wonderful in uniform. He was in the Black Watch of which his aunt Queen Elizabeth was Colonel-in-Chief. John was particularly close to her, and when, in the early months of the war, she visited the regiment's Perth depot she had a poignant encounter with him. She had never seen him in uniform before and wrote to Queen Mary: 'It gave me such a shock to see John in his Black Watch uniform, for he suddenly looked exactly like my brother Fergus who was killed at Loos [in the First World War] and in the same regiment. It was uncanny in a way and desperately sad to feel that all that ghastly waste is starting again at the bidding of a lunatic'.

Five years later, a strange, gaunt figure returned from Germany. We all met him in London and had a celebratory dinner at Buckingham Palace. John had been taken prisoner at St Valery, along with most of the 51st Highland Division at the time of Dunkirk. The 1st Battalion was cut off and forced to surrender near Abbeville after fierce fighting. Only nine men and one officer escaped. By 12 June all fighting had ceased. The officer prisoners were separated from their men, which caused my brother great concern. John, in a contingent of 2500 prisoners, marched 220 miles in fourteen days from northern France to a railhead in Holland, subsisting on a bowl of soup a day, dandelions, marigolds and acorn coffee. They slept in their clothes, sometimes huddled together in open fields under driving rain. It was very cold at night and they stripped greatcoats from the bodies of dead soldiers by the roadside. The French people in the villages they passed smuggled them scraps of food and fruit, having heard by bush telegraph that *lés Anglais* were passing through. In Holland boy scouts bought them cakes and honey. Their destination was Munich and Oflag VIIC. Thereafter John spent five-and-a-half years in captivity. In the later stages of the war he was incarcerated in Colditz Castle, with a group of prisoners known as the 'Prominente', regarded by Hitler of being of special value because of their relationship to prominent Allied figures. The group included Giles Romilly, the nephew of Winston Churchill; Michael Alexander, a relative of Field Marshal Alexander;

Viscount Lascelles, the King's nephew; George Haig, the son of Earl Haig, the British First World War commander, and Charles Hopetown, the eldest son of the Marquess of Linlithgow, the then Viceroy of India.

I have preserved John's letters, always written in pencil on German provided POW forms, from various Oflags. I have also kept his own typewritten detailed account of his final days as a prisoner. A mural John painted is still on the walls of Colditz Castle. The Nazis, faced with defeat, grabbed at any bargaining ace they could pull from their sleeves. My brother and his fellow 'Prominente' were one such bargaining ace, and he and the other members of the group were shuttled across Germany, from Colditz to Austria, in a bid by the German High Command to avoid their liberation by the rapidly advancing Allies.

Prisoners of war: my brother John is in the back row, second from the left

John's account is set out in full below. My brother described the atmosphere as 'gangster-like' and above anything, he dreaded falling into hands of the the more extreme factions of the SS. If that had happened, the 'Prominente' may not have survived. John's state of mind was not improved when he discovered that Himmler, the head of the SS, was taking a personal interest in the operation. John's account sets out the trials and tribulations and eventual liberation through the intervention of the Swiss ministers, reaching the American lines and freedom:

LAST DAYS OF CAPTIVITY
CHRONICLE OF SPECIAL PRISONERS FROM OFLAG IVC
BY
THE MASTER OF ELPHINSTONE

For some months in Oflag IVC. the Germans had been keeping under special surveillance the small group of officers and one civilian concerning whose further moves this account is written. Under roughly the same conditions was also a group of 13 Polish officers headed by General Bor and consisting of high staff officers captured after the battle of Warsaw. The German camp authorities refused to give explanation of this state of affairs other than by saying that the orders came from 'the highest sources'.

On the night of 12-13 April, at 11.30 pm, we were roused from our beds in the room in which we were locked up every night and told that we and the Polish officers were to be ready to leave in two hours. Armed guards in the passages and courtyards made any reasonable scheme for getting away to a 'hide' impossible, and in due course, at 1.30 am, we were marched out into the waiting buses. The American troops were at this time only some 20 miles away, and reached the camp area 24 hours later. In the morning, we arrived at the fortress of Konigstein on the Elbe, where we were lodged in the German quarters of the camp and allowed no contact with the other prisoners of war in the fortress.

Two members of the party were ill and, after some difficulty, it was agreed by the German Kommandant, after telephoning to Berlin, that these two officers, with one British orderly, should remain there until well. Since we could hear from the fortress the guns on the Front, we all thought it likely that, within a very short time this camp, too, would be liberated — an event which unfortunately took very much longer to materialise than we expected.

Next morning, the rest of the party were motored down through Czechoslovakia, seeing frantic efforts being made on all roads to make road-blocks, anti-tank ditches and weapon-pits. We spent the night at Klattau, and at dawn moved on into Bavaria, and finally stopped outside an internee camp at Laufen, twelve miles north of Salzburg. Our great anxiety was the possibility of being taken out of Wehrmacht (army) hands and as this now seemed probable, a fierce battle of words took place. As senior of the British/American party, I refused to leave the bus or to enter the camp and told the German colonel conducting us that I held him personally responsible for seeing that we were taken to an officers' camp run under army regulations. After some delay, it was agreed that temporarily we could go to the camp of Dutch officer-prisoners ten miles away.

After several days spent with the Dutch officers, who received us with the greatest possible kindness, and gave us every help, we were informed that we were to be removed back to Laufen.

We decided that more extreme measures than protests must be taken, and, accordingly, with the help of two Dutch officers in particular, a hurried scheme was arranged whereby one member of the party and one Dutch officer, should escape by a rope (more than two being unlikely to get out unobserved owing to various difficulties) and the rest of us should be bricked up in a cleverly constructed 'hide' in the wall of the room, previously prepared by the Dutch officers. The Polish officers were unable to join us, and were removed the next day to the internee camp at Laufen. All went well the first night; two civilian members of our party and one Dutch officer succeeded in making a 'get-away' while we remained in the 'hide' hoping that the Germans would presume us all to have escaped when they found the rope left hanging down the outer wall.

We were told later that the German authorities were panic-stricken as they had been informed that they would forfeit their lives if we escaped. 3,000 Germans scoured the countryside and a very thorough search was made inside the camp itself – without any success. On the fourth day, however, presumably suspecting that some of us were still hidden in the camp, they made an even more drastic search – walls, floors and ceilings all being torn up – and eventually the plastered-up entrance to the 'hide' was knocked down and we were pulled out. Under very heavy escort, we were taken to the internee camp at Laufen. Here the German general commanding the Munich area visited the camp, and in the course of an interview, finally gave me his word of honour that we should remain there until the end of the War – a promise repeated in the presence of the Swiss Minister by the German Kommandant the next day. The latter, however, could, or would, give no reason for our detention, apart from all other officer-prisoners, except that it was ordered by Himmler.

All remained quiet until the fall of Munich, and then, with the Americans once more rapidly approaching, the orders were given that we were to move at once — in spite of promises given — into the mountains of the Austrian Tyrol. Two officers, an SS colonel and a Luftwaffe major, were sent by Obergruppenfuhrer and General of SS Berger to conduct us. At 6.30 am we entered the transport, with the colonel fingering his revolver, watching us with a somewhat sinister-looking blonde woman who accompanied him in his car. This was possibly the most trying of all the moves, as the whole scene had a gangster-like atmosphere. We drove through Salzburg, past Berchtesgaden and finally stopped at a Stalag in a remote valley in the Tyrol. We were allowed no contact with the prisoners, who included representatives of most of the allied nations, but were isolated in the German part of the camp.

The representatives of the Swiss Legation (Protecting Power) with admirable and with very reassuring promptitude, followed us and visited the Kommandant within a very few hours of our arrival. Later the Swiss Minister and his staff started on the series of interviews and discussions with the leading German government figures who were in the neighbourhood. This work, which they carried out with wonderful patience and success, was of the utmost difficulty, as the leaders were scattered in remote mountain hamlets, and all roads were choked with army vehicles and personnel.

Finally SS Obergruppenfuhrer Berger, chief, amongst other things, of all prisoner-of-war affairs, agreed to hand us over to the Swiss, and allow them to conduct us through the lines. He did this on his own responsibility and warned the Swiss that other elements of the government would, if they knew, resist his orders and lay hands on us. He therefore sent to the camp a special guard under an SS colonel, armed with every type of weapon, to guard us against the 'other German elements' during the final night of our captivity.

Berger himself came to visit us and in a long and theatrically declaimed speech reiterated, probably for the last time, many of the well-worn phrases of German propaganda together with several revelations of the complete break-up of the German government and people. He then informed us that, owing to this break-up, he felt he was no longer in a position to safeguard us properly and had agreed to hand us over to Swiss protection On leaving, he turned, theatrical to the end, to the German officers in charge of us and, having given his final commands, said: 'Gentlemen, these are probably the last orders I shall give as a high official of the German Third Reich'. We were due to leave at 11 am the next morning. The Swiss Legation attaché, who was to accompany us in his car, arrived early, but for more than three rather tantalizing hours, there was no sign of the German trucks which were to take the party, a fact which caused some anxiety in view of Berger's warnings. At length, however, two other trucks were secured locally, thanks once again to the perseverance of the Swiss attaché, and finally at about 5 pm we set off, each vehicle draped with the Swiss flag, along the densely packed roads. Accompanying us was a SS medical office as personal representative of General Berger.

A STRANGE INTERLUDE

At about 11.30 pm, this officer stopped the convoy in a small village in the mountains, saying that he had orders from General Berger to see that we had food and drink in his headquarters here. We entered a house filled with SS troops, many of them intoxicated, and were shown into an upstairs room where some food and much drink was laid out. In the middle of the meal, the Obergruppenfuhrer once more made a theatrical entry, played the expansive if somewhat nerve-strained host, and again poured out a flood of propaganda and explanation. After some time he gave an order to a SS adjutant, who handed him a scarlet leather case. After yet another speech, he turned to me as senior of the British/American party, and handed me the case as 'a proof of his good feelings'. Inside was an elaborately ornamented pistol of ivory, brass and enamel, with his own signature engraved on the butt.

After this strange interlude, we set off once more. At dawn we passed successfully through the last German post and shortly afterwards were halted, to our joy and relief, by a spearhead force of six American tanks. A few hours later we were most kindly and hospitably welcomed by an American divisional headquarters at Innsbruck. It would be difficult indeed for our party adequately to express our gratitude to the Swiss minister and his staff for all that they did to make the release possible.

* * *

After Queen Elizabeth's death, I was given the task of sorting through her correspondence, and found a letter to my brother John, complete in its envelope, addressed to 'British Prisoner of War N.1186' at OFLAG VII B, which was, inexplicably, never posted. I still have it. It is a wonderful, charming letter, in which she listed all the things John might be able to enjoy once he was free, including inviting a few guns from among his prisoner friends to a shoot in the Highlands and stay at Gannochy. She told him that the very grand butler there, known as 'Lord' Bingley, had, 'wise man', married the cook, and assured John that 'Lady' Bingley would cook for him and his friends 'exquisitely'. Perhaps

Queen Elizabeth, being a sensitive soul, hesitated to send it because she thought a description of pleasures he might never be able to enjoy would make him even more home sick.

My younger brother, Andrew, was in the Cameron Highlanders. A lot of his men came from the Outer Isles and spoke Gaelic, so he went off to live for a short while on the island of Benbecula to learn the language — a notoriously difficult one to master — and I remember him reciting the Lord's Prayer in Gaelic. Andrew, to his chagrin, was found to be medically unfit for active service, due to a heart condition, and was posted to India as ADC to the Viceroy Lord Linlithgow. This was an unbelievable chance for a twenty-one-year-old, but 'Hopey' Linlithgow, as he was known to his friends, resigned in 1943, in the wake of the spreading resistance to British rule, and Andrew came home to be recruited to MI5, through my intervention, sharing rooms with me in Buckingham Palace, when I was working for MI6, as described in the next chapter. He was an accomplished pianist, and, in my view, good enough for the concert circuit, but after the war, he felt impelled towards the Anglican priesthood. He was in a dilemma; was his future to be the piano or the pulpit. Divine providence, however, intervened. One day, sawing wood with a circular electric saw he inadvertently cut off the first finger of his right hand. The decision was therefore made for him and he became a clergyman.

I still managed to escape to Glenmazeran, where we had a keeper called Duncan who taught me a lot about shooting and fishing. He also had other talents which proved useful in a time of shortages, becoming a prominent figure in the local Black Market. I suppose this was very reprehensible, but there were some things one couldn't do without. Duncan could produce an illicit petrol coupon or two and he had a good line in knickers, the old fashioned, elastic round the legs kind, and other little comforts. I don't know whether he was ever rumbled. I hope not, because as far as I was concerned he was performing a public service, although I sometimes wondered whether I was an accessory after the fact. Towards the end of 1941, when I was sixteen, I was sent to a finishing school in Oxford to have my rough edges smoothed. We were supposed to talk French all the time and were allowed to attend lectures being given in the university. With French, a smattering of Italian, and a touch of philosophy, I was considered 'finished', although it has always amazed me that I acquired an education at all. Luckily, I have always devoured books and so perhaps I am largely self-educated.

I was enamoured of a young man called Bill Birch Reynardson who was up at Christ Church. He escorted me to a dance at Windsor Castle, but geography put an end to this potential romance when he left Oxford. I then went off to prepare to earn my living by learning shorthand and typing at the Queen's Secretarial College, which had been evacuated from London to Surrey. I stayed at Windsor Castle, with the Princesses, and caught the bus to Egham every day.

The castle had returned to its original role as a fortress and there was a plan for my cousins to disappear in the event of an invasion. It was, I believe, called the Coats Mission because it was commanded by a high ranking officer called Coats. A hand picked body of officers and men from the Brigade of Guards and the Household Cavalry, equipped with armoured cars, was on twenty-four hour call to take the King and Queen and their daughters to a safe house in the country should the German threat of invasion materialise. I don't think there was much reason to worry about that after 1940, but it was a comforting thought that they were around, until I learned that although the operation probably included the corgis, it did not include me.

Windsor Castle was a bit bleak in those days. Heavy black out curtains made the rooms look gloomy and the furniture was naturally shrouded in dust covers. It seemed to be perpetual twilight. The King and Queen, who came down from London at weekends, observed the food rationing regulations although the rations were supplemented by game birds and venison. The pudding every day was stewed bottled plums, picked from the garden.

In order to save on vital supplies, we were only allowed three inches of water in the bath and the King commanded that a black line be painted as a sort of ablutionary Plimsoll line. It was, of course, impossible actually to regulate this and I'm sure there were many who totally ignored His Majesty's attempt to impose water rationing. Often there were air raids, and the Page would come in, bow, and announce: 'Purple warning, Your Majesty', the signal that the Luftwaffe was zooming in. I remember one particularly heavy attack when we all had to go to the shelter. We were roused in the middle of the night and first taken to the King and Queen's bedroom where I think I saw the King take a revolver from the drawer of his bedside table. It was a defensive precaution, bearing in mind the possibility of an enemy parachute drop aimed at his capture. I know too that Queen Elizabeth practised revolver shooting in the garden of Buckingham Palace, particularly after the Palace was bombed, which meant huge numbers of rats ran free, so she was able to practice on moving targets.

My siblings Jean, John, Elizabeth and Andrew holding me as a baby

We then walked what seemed like miles and miles, down into the bowels of the castle. On the trek Queen Elizabeth absolutely refused to be hurried, despite the efforts of courtiers to persuade her to move faster. Hitler had described her as the most dangerous woman in Europe, after he saw a newsreel clip of her laying a single poppy on a memorial to the Commonwealth dead in the First World War during the state visit to France in 1938, a time when, despite the Munich Agreement, many people believed that war was inevitable. It was a symbolic gesture, as were her dragging feet, typifying her attitude to Nazi aggression. The Fuhrer was not going to force her pace. This did not mean that the raids did not disturb her. At the end of December 1940 she wrote to my sister, Elizabeth, saying: 'I am still just as frightened of bombs and guns going off as I was at the beginning. I turn bright red, and my heart hammers. In fact I'm a beastly coward, but I do believe that a lot of people are, so I don't mind...Down with the Nazis'.

But outside the family she knew that she could not give an inkling that she might be scared. One such occasion was when she had a meeting with Lady Reading, the head of the WVS at Buckingham Palace during a particularly bad raid. The palace had already been bombed and as they talked the explosions got closer and closer. Lady Reading was renowned as a most formidable woman and was obviously not the least concerned.

They were ensconced by the big windows overlooking the garden and Queen Elizabeth rather wanted to suggest that it would be sensible to move a little further away from the possible danger of shattered glass. Lady Reading, however, just went on talking and talking. Afterwards my aunt said that she had to strongly remind herself that she was the Queen of England and couldn't possibly show any fear.

I have many memories of my sojourn at Windsor, and the comings and goings of important figures in the war effort. For instance I met the South African Prime Minister, Jan Christiaan Smuts and I like to think that decades later when I was introduced to Nelson Mandela that I had rounded the circle as far as South African politics were concerned. But for frivolous reasons I particularly remember one summer afternoon when we were having tea on a small terrace overlooking the castle rose garden. A long white tablecloth swept to the ground, and the table was set with a silver kettle, teapot and all the usual paraphernalia. The party comprised the King; the Queen; the Princesses, myself, and my friend Liz Lambart, who, like me, was

Her Majesty Queen Elizabeth The Queen Mother, painted by Sue Crawford

A shooting party, Windsor

Queen Elizabeth and me, 1982

Her Majesty The Queen and me at Balmoral

Queen Elizabeth and me at Pol Vier, Birkhall, c. 1984

Queen Elizabeth and Her Majesty The Queen
on Queen Elizabeth's 76th birthday

Queen Elizabeth and Prince Charles picknicking in Scotland, 1994

Queen Elizabeth at Pol Veir, Birkhall

Princess Margaret at Leoville
Barton October 1994

Queen Elizabeth, my sister Jean and
me at Birkhall, 2000

Her Majesty The Queen and me at Loch Muick, Balmoral

The wedding of my daughter Victoria, 1999. Her Majesty The Queen, Queen Elizabeth, me, Jesse Deans, Victoria and John Pryor, Austen Deans, Marjorie Pryor and Princess Margaret

My 70th birthday party at Buckingham Palace
Michael, me, Simon, Victoria and Annabel

My 80th birthday party, June 12th 2005 – Teddy Tahu Rhodes is singing in the background

With Her Majesty The Queen at Balmoral

With Her Majesty The Queen at Garden House

A family gathering, 2005

Garden House, Windsor

a bridesmaid to Princess Elizabeth. Liz, a daughter of the Earl of Cavan, was sharing my shorthand and typing labours.

Suddenly we heard male voices engaged in transatlantic chatter. The King exclaimed: 'Oh Lord. General Eisenhower and his group are being shown round the castle. I quite forgot. We will all be in full view when they turn the next corner'. It was embarrassing because the little terrace was half way up the castle wall and they would have been clearly seen, but unable to descend or to communicate in any way with the visitors. Thus without another word, and acting as one, the Royal Family dived under the table cloth. Liz and I, our mouths gaping open, followed fast. We stayed there until we thought it safe to reappear. Eisenhower must have been over here planning the D-Day landings at that time. If he and his party had looked up towards the terrace they would have seen a table shaking from the effect of the concerted and uncontrollable giggles of those sheltering beneath it. Years later, on a State Visit to America, the present Queen confessed to the then President Eisenhower about it and he thought it very funny.

I had normal school holidays from the secretarial college and was able to enjoy my usual visits to Balmoral. By then I was seventeen and considered to be sufficiently grown up to be allowed down to dinner. One night I witnessed the Royal Family experiencing the personal tragedy of war. We were sitting there when in the middle of dinner one of the Pages came in and whispered in the ear of His Majesty's Assistant Private Secretary, Sir Eric Mieville. Sir Eric got up and quietly left the room. Minutes later he returned and whispered to the King. The King then left. There was silence around the dining room table. Conversation was impossible. We sat silently, imagining all the possible disasters that could have happened. At length it became impossible to stay there and, with a feeling of relief, the Queen stood up and signalled for us to leave the room. She then hurried to join the King, while we all sat in the drawing room, still shocked into silence. At long last the King and Queen returned, and the King told us that his brother, Prince George, Duke of Kent, who was an RAF Air Commodore, had been killed in a flying accident when his plane crashed into a mountain in northern Scotland. The weather had been vile that day; a low mist, rain and an east wind; the worst flying weather. That evening the King and Queen left for London. Seven days later, after the funeral, the King returned to Scotland and made a pilgrimage to the scene of the tragedy.

There were happier times. Despite the war the King and Queen Elizabeth, particularly the Queen, were absolutely wonderful at making life fun for their daughters and their guests. There was a game called 'kick the tin', customarily played after tea. All the visitors, however grand, had to take part. It involved a great deal of running, climbing in and out of windows and generally causing mayhem. I remember watching Sir Samuel Hoare, the Lord Privy Seal, being made to run like the devil and becoming very hot, bothered and confused. I try and imagine a similar holder of high office doing the same nowadays, and I can't. But Queen Elizabeth was very persuasive.

The membership of the first Balmoral house party for the beginning of the grouse shooting was always the same and included Lord and Lady Eldon and Lord and Lady Salisbury. Lord Salisbury — 'Bobbety' to the Royal Family — was a great statesman, but was fortunate, or unfortunate, depending on your point of view, in having his birthday in the middle week of August. At dinner he would be crowned with staghorn moss and rhymes would be declaimed. Queen Elizabeth was always a leading player in this rather pagan ceremony. During the last stages of dinner we would belt out the latest hit songs. When, she was older, Princess Margaret, who had a satirical wit, would create topical new lyrics for these top of the pops performances. She missed her vocation; she should have been in cabaret.

Often there were four and sometimes six pipers in attendance, circling the table at the end of dinner before heading off down the passage with the pipes dying gently away. The pipers were two gamekeepers, a gardener, a pony man and a gate keeper, kilted and plaided in the grey and red Balmoral Tartan. One piper was well known to imbibe generously before playing and the unsteady pattern of his march, let alone his piping, caused a lot of secret amusement. Before dinner, one jolly evening, Magdalen Eldon, a well known practical joker, did some art work on the white marble statue of Queen Victoria's beloved Prince Albert, which stood in the corridor outside the drawing room. She applied lipstick, rouge and mascara and the Prince Consort looked awful. The King was clearly not too distressed by this, although Victoria, had she known would have been furious. It took many hours of hard work to erase the damage, but Albert once scrubbed down resumed his former air of inscrutable benevolence. These dinners were, however, not, without their formality. When the Queen rose to lead the ladies out, they in turn stopped at the door and made a low curtsey to the King, which he acknowledged with a bow to each one. That doesn't happen now, of course, as it is the Queen herself who leads the ladies out.

At Balmoral the male members of the Royal Family wear the grey and red Balmoral tartan, designed by Queen Victoria and Prince Albert in the 1850s. It was here that I learned my first lesson in the male anatomy. My mentor was the King's younger brother, the Duke of Gloucester, who unfortunately never quite mastered the correct technique of adjusting the kilt when seated.

Years and years later, at the annual Ghillies Ball at Balmoral, the Resident Factor, who is responsible for the management of the Balmoral estate, kilted of course, was sitting out one of the reels on a leather covered banquette. It was perhaps a little over warm and when the Queen approached, he had to struggle to rise — slowly and with obvious difficulty. His bare bottom had stuck to the leather and there was an unexpressed 'ouch'. He told me afterwards: 'I only hope that Her Majesty thought the tears in my eyes were due to the emotion I felt at being addressed by her'.

CHAPTER FOUR

Secret Army

I tip-toed into the world of work with a difference when I finished my shorthand and typing course. I wanted to 'do my bit', as the saying then went and join the Women's Royal Naval Service, the WRNS, but for a now forgotten reason I found myself in MI6 as a small cog in the shadowy world of espionage. It was all dreadfully hush-hush, and for an impressionable eighteen-year old tremendously mysterious. I reported each day with some trepidation to an office disguised as 'Passport Control' near St James's Park underground station. Perhaps it was 'Passport Control' on the ground floor, but upstairs we were MI6. The big chief, 'M' to James Bond fans, hid behind the letter 'C'. He wrote in green ink, and God-like powers were attributed to him by us underlings. Years later I was told that the spy Kim Philby had at one time been in line for the 'C' job. He would probably have written in red ink. But my boss, a Major Maufe, was an excessively dull character. When forced to make a rare venture into the social circuit he attended a smart cocktail party given by people he didn't know, he introduced himself by saying: 'I'm Maufe', as in 'Orf'. The invariable response was: 'Oh, so sorry you couldn't stay longer'. Thereafter things became a touch confused.

My department co-ordinated the work of our secret agents in the Near East. They all seemed to travel by caique. Then I went to work for the Depury Director DD/Admin, with a very nice lady whose husband was an agent and I remember her distress when he broke both ankles dropping by parachute into occupied France. With the ever vigilant Gestapo on their tail, mobility could mean the difference between life and death to our agents. I never learnt his fate, but I hope so much that he survived. One of my daily tasks was to read every single message transmitted by our spies all over the world. It was fascinating, but frightening too. I knew all about Germany's war time race for nuclear weapons being conducted at their heavy water plant in Norway and it was a tremendous relief when in 1943 a team of British trained Norwegian commandos succeeded in blowing up the plant. The Special Operations Executive described it as one of the most daring and successful acts of sabotage in the Second World War.

I was also aware of the Peenemunde project on the Baltic coast where the Germans were developing their new secret weapon, a rocket to be launched on London and the south east and the building of the rocket launching sites in Holland and France, with the aim of bringing Britain to its knees. It was to be Hitler's last throw. The evidence had been brought to Winston Churchill by his son-in-law Duncan Sandys who, having been badly wounded in the battle for Norway in 1940 had been made responsible for the search for and the discovery of secret weapons. My husband, Denys Rhodes, later worked for Duncan Sandys when he was involved in thee foundation of the European Movement, a forerunner of the European Community.

In 1943, it was useful, but scary, to know that the V1 and V2 rockets were stoking up long before they actually fell on us. Forewarned was forearmed, and one of the girls with whom I worked and shared a flat with in Chelsea went to bed every night wearing a tin hat. She failed in her attempt to persuade me to take the same precaution. I thought it was carrying personal safety too far. When the V1 onslaught began it was frightening, mostly because of its total unpredicatability – its fall being decided by its petrol tank. The moment one heard the engine noise cease, one knew it had started its descent. But defiantly nicknaming these death carrying projectiles 'Doodle Bugs' helped to allay the fear and they became just another horror to get used to. I had first hand experience of this one Sunday, in June 1944, when I was on duty in 'Passport Control' and heard a V1 cut out. It sounded very nearly overhead and stupidly I craned out of the window to see where it would fall. A rather crusty old colonel saw me as he was passing and rugby tackled me down on to the floor, a rescue operation accompanied by some round curses. That was the rocket which hit the Guards' Chapel, in Wellington Barracks, barely a hundred yards away. It was the middle of the morning service. Sixty three servicemen and women and fifty-eight civilians were killed. The V2s were even more frightening as they were silent and gave absolutely no warning of their approach. One could, however, hear the roar of their approach, after they had landed, like an express train, but then of course it was too late for so many innocent victims.

I have often reflected since those momentous days, on how curiously adaptable human beings are. At the time all the dangerous situations thrust upon us during the war strangely didn't actually seem dangerous; just commonplace. I remember after a weekend in the country arriving back at Victoria station, just after an air raid, and picking my way through piles of shattered glass and rubble along streets with flaming buildings on each side. One just took it in one's stride. It was just as well, of course, otherwise life would have been completely intolerable. But beside the air raids and work there was play. The theatres and cinemas remained open and there were lots of young men around, all in uniform of course. They looked so handsome in their dress 'Blues' and as often as not we would end up at the 400 club, in Leicester Square. It was dark; smoky and romantically mysterious. There was a tiny square dance floor on which we smooched around, cheek to cheek, imagining ourselves in love.

I had two weeks leave a year and usually headed home to Scotland. The trains were slow and packed with servicemen. I would sit bolt upright all night in a third class compartment, with the windows blacked out and covered with some sticky protective material in case they were blasted in or out during a raid. The only illumination was a dim blue light in the roof. At Carberry I found that my mother had risen to the challenge of supplementing the meagre rations with home grown recipes. We ate stewed nettles both as vegetables and in soup, melted down rose hips and very old eggs preserved in something called 'waterglass'. Each adult was entitled under the strict food rationing regime to two small meat cutlets a week; about four ounces of butter and the same amount of sugar. Fruit was only the home grown variety and everywhere one looked one could see flower gardens turned into vegetable patches and allotments. We were luckier in the country than people living in the towns. We could always shoot rabbits or pigeons and many a hen past its laying prime would find its way to the family table. It was a long way from the lavishness of our pre-war picnics and dinners when my parents entertained house parties during the shooting season, but most people, particularly the children, seemed remarkably healthy. Childhood obesity was not then a problem.

Back in London, the girls with whom I worked and lived with, and I, were overwhelmingly affected by the drama of our jobs and were only too ready to see spies lurking round every corner. Those were the days when people, unbelievably now, regularly reported spotting parachuting nuns, every single sister a spy of course. Elizabeth Lambart and I lived as paying guests in a house in Chelsea. Our landlord spoke with a heavy foreign accent and limped, although we once caught him running up the stairs. He was often away and something of an enigma. Was he, I wondered, transmitting to Berlin. He would offer us lifts to work in the morning — how did he get the petrol for his car — and we went to extraordinary lengths to convince him that we worked in a totally different part of London. We were convinced that he was a spy. We even went as far as reporting him to MI5, although I never found out what happened to him. In retrospect I hope it wasn't anything too serious.

Later in the war my mother managed to engineer both my brother Andrew and me into Buckingham Palace as lodgers. I would think that it probably would not have needed much more than a telephone call to her sister, the Queen. Our new home was wonderfully convenient, because it was, for me only a short walk across the park to 'Passport Control'. We had a bedroom each, a sitting room and a bathroom all on the second floor and a housemaid's pantry as our kitchen. There was a small electric cooker, but no fridge. I thought it would be a good idea to utilise the window ledge and so put our milk bottles out there to keep them cool, only to bring down on my head the wrath of the Master of the Household, a dear old boy called Sir Piers Legh, who gave me the most fearsome ticking off for defacing the architectural purity of the palace facade; as if he didn't have other things to worry about. The palace had already been bombed nine times, and there were all those refugee royals passing through, like Queen Wilhelmina of the Netherlands, who having narrowly escaped capture by the invading Germans, arrived with little more than what she stood up in and a tin hat.

Our window overlooked the forecourt and I don't suppose my domestic improvisations enhanced the Changing of the Guard. Our great culinary forté was a stockpot which we kept going for months on end and in which we would pop whole pigeons. There were plenty of them to be had, and cheap at 2s 6d (12.5p) each. I imagine that Trafalgar Square was rather depleted. Once we actually invited the King and Queen to dinner — imagine in a house maid's pantry. The horrified staff was convinced that Their Majesties would succumb to food poisoning. The King's Page, the tall and elegant Mr Hailey, was particularly distressed about His Majesty slumming in his own palace, and appeared, unasked, to check over our arrangements, which he found highly unsatisfactory. Buckingham Palace was of course the most prestigious address in town, but it did deter some of my after-dark escorts. The conversations with these hopeful gallants would run something like this: 'Can I see you home?'... 'How Kind'... 'Where do you live?'.... 'Buckingham Palace'... 'Oh REALLY', with an emphasis on the 'REALLY'... 'But where do you live?'... 'Honestly, Buckingham Palace'. Unfortunately my connection with the big house at the top of the Mall sometimes dashed my chances of romance. My escorts had to leave me at the Palace railings, where I still had to get past the soldiers and policemen.

I was twenty in 1945. VE Day was a euphoric moment. I was still at the Palace and that evening we had a huge party. My eldest brother, John, who had been a prisoner of war, was there and a gang of us, including the two Princesses, were given permission by the King and Queen to slip away anonymously and join the rejoicing crowds on the streets. This sort of freedom was unheard of as far as my cousins were concerned. There must have been about sixteen of us and we had as escort, the King's Equerry, a very correct Royal Navy captain in a pin striped suit, bowler hat and umbrella. No one appeared less celebratory, perhaps because he took his guardian responsibilities too seriously. Princess Elizabeth was in uniform, as a subaltern in the Auxiliary Transport Service – the ATS. She pulled her peaked cap well down over her face to disguise her much photographed image, but a Grenadier among the party positively refused to be seen in the company of another officer, however junior, who was improperly dressed. My cousin didn't want to break King's Regulations and so reluctantly she agreed to put her cap on correctly, hoping that she would not be recognised. Miraculously she got away with it.

London had gone mad with joy. We could scarcely move; people were laughing and crying; screaming and shouting and perfect strangers were kissing and hugging each other. We danced the Conga, a popular new import from Latin America; the Lambeth Walk and the Hokey-Cokey, and at last fought our way back to the Palace, where there was a vast crowd packed to the railings. We struggled to the front joining in the yells of 'We want the King; we want the Queen'. I rather think the Equerry got a message through to say that the Princesses were outside, because before long the double doors leading onto the balcony were thrown open and the King and Queen came out, to be greeted by a rising crescendo of cheers, to which their daughters and the rest of us contributed. It was a view of their parents that the Princesses had never before experienced and for all of us young people it was the grand finale to an unforgettable day. I suppose that for the Princesses it was a unique burst of personal freedom; a Cinderella moment in reverse, in which they could pretend that they were ordinary and unknown.

After that life returned to what passed for normal in those days. In mid July the lights went on again 'all over the town', as the popular song had it. After more than two thousand nights of the black out and dim out, Britain was once again ablaze with light, and there was no excuse for bumping into trees or each other in the dark, drunk or sober. Many people listened on the wireless to the news of the continuing war against Japan, culminating in the ultimate horror of atom bombs vaporising Hiroshima and Nagasaki, on 6 and 9 August 1945. There has since been a revisionist view of those two raids, but, I think at the time the great mass of the people, weary of war, were overwhelmingly relieved that it was at last ending and were not overly concerned at the time about the moral argument. That was to come later. Four days after the second raid Japan surrendered unconditionally to the Allies. Prince Philip of Greece, second in command of the destroyer *HMS Whelp*, was present in Tokyo Bay for the formal Japanese surrender.

Back to VE Day and we were all out on the streets in full party mood. It was yet another riot of song and dance and once again I was with the Princesses. I can't remember exactly what we got up to, and so the Queen has provided me with an *aide memoire* taken from her diary entries for that time. She starts on 6 May 1945: 'Heard that John and George free and safe!' The exclamation mark probably expresses her pleasure at the return from captivity

68

of my brother John and her paternal cousin, Viscount Lascelles, the elder son of Mary, the Princess Royal, and the Earl of Harewood. Then on 7 May: 'After tea saw John and George who flew back today. John just the same'. On VE Day, 8 May: 'PM announced unconditional surrender. Sixteen of us went out in crowd, cheered parents on balcony. Up St J's St, Piccadilly, great fun', followed on 9 May: 'Out in crowd again — Trafalgar Square, Piccadilly, Pall Mall, walked simply miles. Saw parents on balcony at 12.30 am — ate, partied, bed 3 am!'

There is a gap until 14 August when she recorded the Prime Minister announcing the complete surrender of Japan, followed on 15 August: 'VJ Day. Out in crowd, Whitehall, Mall, St J St, Piccadilly, Park Lane, Constitution Hill, ran through Ritz. Walked miles, drank in Dorchester, saw parents twice, miles away, so many people' and finally, on 16 August: 'Out in crowd again. Embankment, Piccadilly. Rained, so fewer people. Congered into house [a reference to Buckingham Palace and that rather wild dance]...Sang 'till 2 am. Bed at 3 am!'

My cousins were obviously having the time of their lives. Meanwhile I had been making occasional forays to Windsor where the Queen arranged rather more sedate small dances for her daughters, attended by young Guards' officers stationed at the castle and in the town's barracks. Queen Mary, rather wryly, called these boys 'the bodyguard'. Princess Elizabeth dutifully waltzed, fox-trotted and quick stepped, and engaged her partners in small talk, but she was waiting for one man to come home from the war. She had been enamoured of Prince Philip of Greece from an early age. I've got letters from her saying: 'It's so exciting. Mummy says that Philip can come and stay when he gets leave'. She never looked at anyone else. She was truly in love from the very beginning.

With total peace came some sobering statistics which told the price of victory and defeat. I read that over 55 million people were killed, from all sides. Then there were the spine chilling images filmed when the concentration camps were liberated. A world food shortage brought back the return of rationing on a near war time basis and there were long queues at food shops. The winter of 1947 blew in with heavy snow storms and sub-zero temperatures, meaning serious fuel shortages and power cuts. A frozen Britain lived and worked by candlelight. So the wedding of Princess Elizabeth to Philip Mountbatten, newly minted as a British subject, in November that year, brightened our austerity ridden post war world. This time I was on the Palace balcony myself, as a bridesmaid, standing between Princess Margaret and another cousin, Diana Bowes-Lyon, gazing down on the crowds, who from that distance seemed Lilliputian. Our dresses were designed by Norman Hartnell. They were of ivory satin and net silk tulle, embroidered with syringa flower motifs. We bridesmaids didn't have a girl's party on the wedding eve as they do now, but we did, on the wedding day itself, have an evening party hosted by the best man, David Milford Haven. He was perhaps not the most attentive of hosts and it was not a great success: anyway we were probably all too exhausted.

There were eight bridesmaids, the traditional number for a royal bride. We flitted round the red carpeted corridors of the Palace waiting for the cars to take us to Westminster Abbey and I remember waving to the crowds. It was very exciting but I was shocked to learn that the price of a window view in buildings overlooking the processional route could cost up to ten guineas a head, a lot of money in those days. I know that there were some last minute crises. The bride's bouquet disappeared. A footman remembered taking it in and bringing it upstairs, but no one had seen it since. With the panic at its height he suddenly recalled putting it in a cool cupboard to keep it fresh — and there it was.

Then Princess Elizabeth decided she wanted to wear the double string of pearls which had been a personal wedding gift from her father and mother. The pearls could not be found either, but someone remembered that they had been sent over with the rest of the wedding presents for public display at St James's Palace, half a mile away. The Princess's Private Secretary, Jock Colville, was dispatched poste haste and he commandeered the car of the King of Norway almost before he got out of it. At St James's the detectives guarding the gifts thought he was telling them a tall story, but after some while he convinced them and returned clutching the pearls with only minutes to spare. There was a third mishap. The frame of the sun-ray tiara lent to the Princess by the Queen, as 'something borrowed' snapped as it was being fitted on her head, and the Crown Jeweller who was standing by in case of any emergency rushed to his workroom with a police escort and repaired it just in time. Regrettably I lost my lovely dress in a house move.

I left my M16 job soon after the end of the war, and thereafter spent a lot of time trying to find new and interesting employment. Eventually I pulled off an interview with the fledgling European Movement. I was invited to lunch at the Jardin des Gourmets restaurant in Soho to meet my putative employers. One introduced himself as Denys Rhodes. It was the start of an exciting and romantic adventure which was to take me to the top of the world — and down again.

CHAPTER FIVE

Love and Marriage

Denys Rhodes was six years older than me and very much a man of the world. His father, Major Arthur 'Tahu' Rhodes, of the Grenadier Guards was a New Zealander, a member of one of the earliest settler families, once the owners of vast tracts of land on South Island. Denys was born in Ireland where his mother's family had roots in the Irish judiciary; the higher reaches of the Church of Ireland and a touch of the 'Beerage' because of their links with the aristocratic Guinness brewing family. My mother-in-law, Helen, known as Nellie, was the daughter of Lord Plunket, who had been Governor of New Zealand during the reign of King Edward VII. He bore the standard of the Dominion of New Zealand at the coronation of King George V. Helen, whose mother was a daughter of the 1st Marquess of Dufferin and Ava, and 'Tahu' the Maori name with which he was christened, met while Lord Plunket was at Government House.

Denys was sent to Harrow where he was thought rather clever and then to Grenoble University. As a young man Denys joined the Westminster Rifles, part of the TA and when the Second World War broke out he enlisted in the 60th Rifle Brigade, fighting across North Africa and Italy, where he was wounded and brought home. After he was demobilised he was taken on by Randolph Churchill, the son of the war time premier, Winston Churchill, as a sort of unofficial ADC for a lecture tour of America. Randolph was a successful writer but not so successful a politician. They had met during the war. Randolph has often been portrayed as having had a serious drinking problem, and it was rather a kill or cure trip. They survived many misadventures, dug each other out of several holes, but ended up on reasonably amicable terms. Denys helped him in his campaign when he contested the Devonport parliamentary constituency in 1950. He was narrowly defeated and it was his fourth failed attempt to get into parliament.

Soon after our marriage Denys and I were invited to spend a weekend with Randolph, and one of my recollections was at tea time encountering him, still in his dressing gown, sitting at the tea table, drowning whatever sorrows he had in whisky. My austere Scottish soul was shocked. That Sunday we were invited to lunch with Winston at Chequers, and drove there in our car. Randolph's daughter, Arabella, who was then a small child, sat in the back and was comprehensively sick on the way. On that hot July day, over sixty years ago, we arrived to meet her grandfather, the Prime Minister, smelling faintly of sick and looking rather pea-green — not a good beginning. Arabella later took up charity work and became co-founder of the Glastonbury festival.

There was a large gathering on the terrace and Randolph lost his head, introducing me to everybody as Lady Margaret Rhodes, which, of course, I wasn't. Jock Colville, who by then had become Winston's private secretary, and who knew several members of my family, took me in tow to correct this social solecism, but made it worse, re-introducing me as Mrs Elphinstone, which again I wasn't. At lunch I — the lady seemingly with three names — was made to sit between Winston and his son. My attempts at conversation with the Prime Minister were received with grunts and finally Winston and Randolph had a row across me. It was a day I wished had never happened. This was at the beginning of Queen Elizabeth II's reign and I remember being told that when Winston attended his first prime ministerial audience with her she was so over awed at being in the presence of the great man that she hardly dared to speak. He, on the other hand, was overcome with emotion and wept tears of chivalric adoration.

After his spell with Randolph Churchill, Denys, like so many ex-servicemen, was in an employment limbo. He did various jobs, including being a private detective and working for a sewage company: I never enquired too much about that. But when I first met him he was in the more salubrious surroundings of the embryonic European Movement, founded in 1947 by Duncan Sandys. Its aim was a united Europe and its first major achievement was the setting up of the Council of Europe in 1949. But, however noble its aims, I formed a less than flattering view of the organisation during my interview in the Jardin des Gourmets. I could never fathom the reason why the Frenchman, Jean Paul and Denys thought it would be hilariously funny to pose as being gay. It was fifty years or so since Oscar Wilde had been imprisoned for homosexuality, but same sex relationships were still illegal and men went to prison if they were caught out. But I needed a job and what was on offer sounded interesting. I was taken on as a personnel officer and for the first few weeks sat in Denys' office, where he was supposed to be showing me the ropes. In fact he spent most of his time on the telephone chatting up what seemed to be a harem of girl friends, which at least assured me about his sexual tastes. Consequently he taught me very little about my duties, although I learnt something about him.

My first European challenge was an important conference in Brussels, for which I had overall responsibility for its smooth running. I was terrified and for weeks before I hardly slept, fretting about all the things that could go wrong. Figures like Jean Monnet, who was busy transforming Europe, haunted my dreams. To my relief the conference went rather well, but my memories of it are more coloured by the après conference activities, particularly the drama sparked off by our unstable accountant, who among other diversions took the night off to go to the cinema to see a frightening film, called 'The Snake Pit'. It tipped him over the edge and he returned to our hotel in the middle of the night in a right old state, racing round the floors stark naked, screaming 'Look out, the snakes are here!'

We were due to leave the next day on the Dover ferry and somehow the poor man had to be got home to England. We locked him in his bedroom and a doctor was called, who sedated him. He called again the next morning and gave him some knock out pills, assuring us that he would definitely remain unconscious until the ferry docked, when we would be met by an ambulance. As luck would have it a storm blew up and the sailing was delayed for several hours. Denys and I were horrified at the prospect of travelling with a fully conscious madman for the whole cross Channel voyage. But that was what happened, and the only thing we could do was to lash him with ropes to his bunk and take turns in watching him.

It was an enormous relief when we delivered him into the hands of the ambulance crew and to recover we went to Denys' mother's house near West Malling in Kent. She was a widow and a delight to know, with a mop of grey birds nest hair and with a Turkish cigarette permanently fixed between her lips. She had some very down to earth habits; she drank pink gins with reckless abandon and always sat with her legs wide apart, so that the assembled company were treated to a good view of her knickers. She had five children all of whom in their different way were extraordinary, some of them with bags of artistic and acting talent. I was totally seduced by this. I had always thought that the Elphinstones were a very close family, but compared with the Rhodes brood and the Plunkets, we were inhibited and reserved. Perhaps it was a Scottish trait.

The youngest Rhodes daughter, Pam, was vivacious and full of laughter and I was astonished when she went off to be a nun. She used to wear plus-fours under her habit to keep her legs warm in winter. In the end she jumped over the wall, as the saying goes about holy sisters who change their minds and ended up in Zululand working for the Mothers' Union, the Church of England organisation, until sadly she died of cancer. Teddy, the youngest son was a Grenadier, like his father. After he was demobbed at the end of the war he returned home and was careless enough to get one of his mother's maids pregnant. There was a family panic and he was banished to New Zealand. The unfortunate maid, or fortunate depending on your point of view, followed and family pressure forced him to make an honest woman of her. They were an example of the social mores of the time and I can't imagine such an arrangement now.

My mother-in-law had three brothers and two sisters. The eldest brother, also Teddy, the 6th Baron Plunket and his beautiful wife Dorothe were both killed in an air crash in America in 1938. They were on their way to California to a party being given in their honour by William Randolph Hearst, the newspaper tycoon, at his extravaganza of a mansion at San Simeon. His career inspired the

Orson Welles film 'Citizen Kane'. Teddy and Dorothe were part of the *jeunesse d'orée* of London between the wars. They were great friends of the present Queen's parents when they were still Duke and Duchess of York. They left three orphaned sons, the youngest only five. My mother-in-law took them under her wing and installed them, with her five children, in a flat in Eaton Mansions. The Plunket children arrived with their nanny and their own butler. The Rhodes' family nanny Mrs Appleby was also in residence. During the Second World War London blitz she would work herself into a panic because she was convinced that the Germans would bomb Regent's Park Zoo, and that the lions would escape and unerringly make their way to Eaton Mansions, get into the lift and exit at the top floor with the intention of eating her. Unbelievable really, that anyone could be so deliciously eccentric.

Patrick, the eldest Plunket boy, succeeded to the Barony when he was scarcely fifteen. Four-years younger than Denys, he ended up a Lieutenant Colonel in the Irish Guards and was successively Equerry to George VI and Queen Elizabeth II and was appointed Deputy Master of the Household in the year after the coronation. He combined, to the Queen's advantage, a love and knowledge of art. With an awareness of people's eccentricities, he was adept at arranging a seating plan which kept everyone happy. That was something that required an intimate knowledge of all the participants. He was Denys' first cousin and I remember him as delightful and good humoured, always ready to laugh at any joke and not the least a stuffed shirt. He had known the Queen since adolescence and combined an older brother role with that of a close friend and courtier. She minded very much when he died from cancer aged only fifty-one in 1975, with so much more to give.

Denys was amusing, witty, six feet tall and handsome, although not in a chocolate box way. Unfortunately he was penniless. It didn't seem to matter to me at the time. He first kissed me in a taxi going round Hyde Park Corner, which felt comforting and nice, but I was so surprised that I did absolutely nothing. We started going out to dinner and then to clubs where we could dance, including the 400, the top nightclub of the day. The relationship grew into a serious love affair, but there was a major draw back. Denys was married. His wife was the actress Rachel Gurney, whom he had married in 1945. They were unhappy together and by the time I met him they were living apart. They decided to divorce and began the convoluted process, very common in those days, which involved the husband booking into a hotel and paying a tart to be found in bed with him in the morning, there to be conveniently discovered by a private eye who would give the necessary evidence. For some mysterious reason this plan did not get off the ground. They were in a marital limbo and time was ticking by. Denys and I were still working together and marriage was looming larger and larger on the horizon. I couldn't imagine any other way than being married in church. Denys was advised that he should try for an annulment. The date for the hearing was some months ahead and when it finally arrived I spent the day waiting with my friend Liz Lambart. When it was all over Denys picked me up and we drove down to his family in Kent. I know no details of what went on but he was granted the annulment.

Rachel, who was lovely to look at and talented, became a very successful actress and is probably best remembered for her role as Lady Marjorie Bellamy in the television period drama 'Upstairs

Downstairs'. Eventually she was written out of the series and the method chosen was to send her down with the *Titanic*. I seem to remember her giving up her place in one of the last lifeboats to her maid. Rachel died in 2001 and I still keep very much in touch with Sharon, her daughter with Denys, who is my stepdaughter and my four step grandchildren. I love them all including Sharon's husband Simon Gough, son of the actor Michael Gough. They lead a delightfully chaotic life in Norfolk and Sharon and my daughter Victoria are close chums.

The annulment hearing had been before an ecclesiastical court and the whole thing had been a great strain for everyone concerned. But at last it was over and Denys was a free man whose first marriage did not count in the eyes of the law. It meant that we could go ahead and make wedding plans. I suppose, in my parents' view, he was not the most suitable bridegroom. For instance, he did not have any inheritance to look forward to but they could see how much I loved him. On 31 July 1950 we were married in St Margaret's, Westminster, with a reception afterwards in Londonderry House, the London residence of the Marquess of Londonderry, who was a distant relative of Denys on his mother's side. Princess Margaret was one of the bridesmaids, but Princess Elizabeth was absent as she was due to give birth to her second child, Princess Anne. She wrote to me on my wedding morning saying how much she was thinking of me. 'You must be so thankful', she said, 'that the great day has arrived at last and I am sure it will be a very happy one for you. I can't really wish you any greater happiness than I have found myself in being married, and I hope that after all the troubles and difficulties your joy with Denys will be extra specially wonderful.'

My wedding dress was of white brocade and I wore the Elphinstone tiara. My dress was made by a Miss Ford who had an establishment just off Bond Street; my mother had had her clothes made by her for years and so she thought it would be sensible if we used her services. I had three other adult bridesmaids; two friends from my teens, Jeannine and Marigold Bridgman and my cousin Diana Bowes-Lyon, as well as two little girls, my nieces Jenny Hambro and Susan Wills.

The King and Queen attended, which was especially important to me, because the King was my Godfather. There were huge crowds in Parliament Square and for the first time in my life I became, in that much overworked present day description, a celebrity. The whole day went by in a blur of hymns and music; champagne, voices; people, people, people and clouds of confetti. We caught the night train to Edinburgh, where the Carberry chauffeur met us with a car we had been lent by my father. We drove to Birkhall which had been lent to us by the King and Queen, who had also hired a cook for us for the first part of our honeymoon. I had a tremendous affection for the old house, which held many happy childhood memories for me and we had a wonderfully peaceful time. Then we set off to the south of France, where Patrick Plunket had rented a villa, perched on top of a hill, high above the Mediterranean. We had another blissful two weeks there and I learnt to gamble in the local casino. The green roulette tables fascinated me and with beginner's luck I actually made money. For a while I fostered the illusion that a casino was as good as a bank.

We returned to London, only to repack our bags to set sail for New Zealand for my introduction to Denys' relations on the other

Our wedding

Wedding day: Among this group are the King and Queen, the Duke of Edinburgh, Princess Margaret, my parents and my mother-in-law

side of the world. We made landfall at Christchurch after five whole weeks at sea. There was a tremor of excitement at the arrival of Queen Elizabeth's niece, and much to the amusement of Denys' aunt Maire Hutton and his cousins, we had to be photographed and interviewed by the press. Auntie Maire, the sister of 'Tahu' Rhodes was married to a sheep farmer called George Hutton, who had been Lord Plunket's ADC when he was Governor of New Zealand. They were a wonderful couple and it was a deliciously eccentric household. They had dreaded my arrival, expecting a posh 'Pom' but they soon discovered that their fears were groundless. Auntie Maire was large and untidy and always wore big felt hats, crammed on to her head at any old angle. She darned the heels of her stockings with whatever coloured wool came to hand.

George VI, Denys's mother and Queen Elizabeth at our wedding reception

They had no help in the house and Uncle George did his own washing in a bucket of cold water. Soap didn't enter into this rudimentary laundry. It felt like there was mutton for breakfast, lunch and tea. We herded the sheep, riding pensioned off polo ponies, fished, shot and explored, sleeping in the back of a van we shipped out from England. We also went into the barely explored areas in the deep south of South Island. This meant a sixteen mile trek up a river carrying our kit, crossing smaller rivers supported by two lines of wire, one for our feet and the other for our hands. It was a hair-raising experience when the rivers were in flood.

Our home for ten days was a one room wooden shack shared with our guide and fellow shooter. It was, in retrospect, an odd way of spending a honeymoon. Each day we climbed through virgin forest to reach the bare hilltops where the deer roamed. It was tough work and Denys succumbed to a knee injury so I went off alone. One day I heard a stag roaring not far away. I roared back, having been taught to do so by our family stalkers. The stag took the bait and approached at an angry and inquisitive trot. I shot him and then skinned him with my not very sharp pen knife, in the way I had learnt by watching the stalkers at home. It was something of a feat. Deer were regarded as pests in sheep rearing country and culling was encouraged and organised officially by state governments. A dollar bounty was the going rate for just a tail and obviously much more for a whole skin. I reckoned I was entitled to at least ten dollars, but did not claim it.

But being the niece of the Queen Consort of New Zealand had its obligations — or drawbacks. We were invited by an organisation glorying in the name of the Pioneer Women of New Zealand to a reception in our honour in Christchurch. The very thought of it sent a chill down my spine, but there was no possibility of refusal, however polite. It was a memorably ghastly event and to my dismay we were greeted by a pipe band which preceded us up the drive of a large suburban house where the rituals were to be staged. The gathering included all the great and the good of South Island, brought to order by the forceful President, a Miss Wigley, who made a speech of welcome. Her best friend, whose name I can't remember, was in attendance. In the middle of the discourse the 'best friend' turned round to do some vital thing she had forgotten. The Wigley barked at her: 'Don't turn your back on royalty'. The ultimate embarrassment was the line up, when all the guests shook our hands and either bowed or curtseyed, probably after a rehearsal conducted by the President. The cousins, acting as sub royalty for the day, clustered in the background doubled up with laughter, but fortunately the Wigley, who by then was in ecstasy, failed to notice.

We returned home in June 1951. Our honeymoon, extraordinary though it may seem these days, had lasted nearly a year. We looked at various houses and found in those days that prices dropped like a stone when you looked in the south west. We fell in love with a rather dilapidated former rectory called Uplowman near Tiverton which had been used by American troops during the war. My darling father bought the house for us for £8,500. I had my first baby, Annabel in February 1952 in London. She decided to arrive late at night and with labour increasing we set off for the hospital in North London via Hyde Park. We swished in through the gate at the top of Exhibition Road, but to our horror, not least that of the expectant mother, we found the gate at the other end firmly shut. It was an awful moment; was my baby to be born in a car? I really needed to get to the hospital and a midwife quickly. Then we had a stroke of fortune; a policeman turned up out of the blue and after giving Denys a short lecture on the opening and closing times of the park, produced a key, wished us well and let us out.

Once I was in the hands of the midwives Denys took himself off to Whites, his club in St James's Street in search of strong drink. This was well before the days of fathers being encouraged to observe every twist and turn of a birth, and personally I did not want him there; it was woman's work, I reckoned. Anyway a delicious little girl duly arrived, perfect in every detail. Back at home Annabel was looked after by a monthly nurse who was very efficient but impossibly grand. She name dropped duchesses she had attended and seemed on intimate terms with many fathers in membership of Whites. We soon acquired a local farmer's daughter as a nursery maid. Three more children arrived, Victoria, born in London in 1953, Simon, in 1957 at home and Michael, in 1960. For a short time we had a nanny and a nursery maid as well as a live-in couple. In those days the wage for a couple was £7 pounds a week and for the nursery maid £3.

Our family home in Devon had thirty acres. The house was three storied, had six bedrooms and a small flat for the married couple who cooked, cleaned and did the gardening. Mr and Mrs Mallet stayed with us for twenty-five years helping us to bring up the children and get on with our lives. We did all this on £3000 a year, which was the income from my Elphinstone marriage settlement.

I had married a very attractive pauper. Denys did not then have a conventional job, but as I had grown up in a household where none of the men actually had salaried positions it seemed the natural order of things and it was good to have the father of the house around all the time. We were incandescently happy and worked like beavers to create a garden. We had a couple of cows and we turned the barn, once the village school, into a deep litter hen house and turkey run rearing the birds for the Christmas trade. We also kept a pig called Percy which lived on the household scraps. When the time came for poor Percy to go to the slaughter house I was distraught. The worst moment was when I went to pick up his corpse from the abbatoir. The dead pigs were hung from their back legs, but I recognised Percy at once and felt even guiltier. I was obviously not cut out to be a livestock farmer.

We loved Uplowman. It was a wonderfully relaxing environment and nobody seemed to mind if I went shopping with my hair in rollers and a cigarette clenched between my teeth. Denys

A family group at Uplowman, painted by T Whidborne

would shut himself away in the summer house and write books in the style of Hammond Innes, published by Longmans. He also went on expeditions for an organisation engaged in desert locust control in the Sudan, Somalia and Kenya and later undertook a search for uranium in Tanzania. His books were largely based on personal experience. One of them, *The Syndicate,* was turned into a rather awful film which seemed to have little relationship to the book. Denys received the princely sum of £500 for the rights and we went to see it at the Electric Cinema in Tiverton. We rather wished we had not been included in the credits.

We also entertained our friends and family. The Queen, Queen Elizabeth and Princess Margaret came for the weekend. Each of them put up their detectives in the local pub, where on one occasion Margaret's policeman made very extensive use of the bar facilities. When the Queen came to stay there was more than usual collaboration with the local constabulary and coppers lurked in the bushes round the house. A footman came to help with the breakfast trays, and the Queen's Dresser was allocated one of the children's rooms, who after eviction had to camp out elsewhere. In the evening we played 'the Game' with one person acting out the title of a book, a saying or a song which had to be guessed by the others.

Memorably one of the other guests, David Stirling who was responsible for the setting up of the Long Range Desert Group, later to become the SAS, was told to act *The Taming of the Shrew* which involved this immensely tall man pretending to be a mouse running up the Queen's skirts. We were crying with laughter but David got quite huffy because we thought his acting was not of Old Vic standards. On the Sunday of the visit we all went to church in the village which delighted our old vicar. I put my foot down at housing Margaret's Dresser and assumed an older cousin role. With our growing family there just wasn't room. Margaret could be a demanding guest, and on one occasion, when she brought her husband, Tony Armstrong Jones, the lavatory seat in their bathroom came apart. I assume that Tony must have sat down heavily. They wanted a replacement installed at once, but it was just not possible over a weekend and we firmly told them so. For a couple whose every whim was pandered to, they took it quite well and there were no more complaints.

In the evening we lightened the mood by playing charades. One of the men dressed up as a woman and unknown to us entered Princess Margaret's bedroom, borrowing a great deal of her make up including her lipstick. He gave a hilarious performance, but it was only much later that Her Royal Highness discovered the depletion of her stock of cosmetics. She failed to see the funny side.

There were no complaints or embarrassing dramas when Queen Elizabeth came. I'm sure she would have much preferred to have spent a quiet weekend at Royal Lodge rather than becoming the pivotal point of a sojourn in our happy go lucky household. I would do my best to make sure that everything ran like clockwork. I would go through every detail of the menus for every meal with Mrs Mallett, attempting to cover every eventuality, and so before my aunt arrived I would bid Mrs Mallett farewell and say, with feeling: 'See you when it's all over'. However despite all my rehearsals, I still managed to receive my aunt wearing gum

Denys at Uplowman, 1960

Left to right: Annabel holding Penny, Michael, Denys, Victoria and Simon in Scotland

boots. Mrs Mallet was horrified, but she recovered enough to have a lovely time, entertaining policemen, footmen and all the guests.

Once when Queen Elizabeth was entertained at Uplowman, it was midsummer and the sheep were making a lot of noise, baa-ing their heads off. In those days we followed the convention of the ladies leaving the gentlemen to their port after dinner. Queen Elizabeth thought they were lingering far too long and marshalled us women outside the dining room window, conducting them in a baa-baa chorus. As the tempo increased in volume the tippling men took the hint and they joined us in the drawing room for coffee.

I have been assured by my children that I am a consummate hostess even when disaster looms. There was one mid-winter occasion when our overworked heating system blew up. The electric fuse box near the kitchen burst into flames and we had to dial 999. The fire brigade arrived and marched through the house in huge muddy boots and quenched the blaze. There was no light and on the heels of the departing firemen the guests arrived for the weekend. We received them by candlelight. We had, of course, dressed for dinner and managed to reorganise the menu. The first course passed in relative peace and then the kitchen hatch opened and Mrs Mallet announced that the cowman's wife had arrived to say that she thought her husband was dead and please, could Mr Rhodes go over and see if he was actually dead. Mr Rhodes declined and told the gardener Mr Mallet to go, as he'd been in the war — so had Denys for that matter but he chose to overlook that qualification — and would know if he was dead. Ten minutes later the hatch opened again and the message was that Mr Mallet thought the cowman was dead, although he had twitched a couple of times. The final request, death having been established, was for Mr Rhodes to go and lay the poor man out. This pleasure, I'm afraid, Denys also declined. The awful thing was that the whole macabre sequence was unbelievably funny and our rather ribald weekend guests were convulsed, save one of them, Lady Waverley, the recently widowed wife of Sir John Anderson, the Second World War Home Secretary, who had been responsible for planting corrugated iron air shelters the length and breadth of the land, known as Anderson shelters, who seemed merely bemused. She wrote to me afterwards saying that perhaps she had been taking death too seriously — which was very tactful of her. Queen Elizabeth would have revelled in the situation if she had been there.

We both used to be asked to Balmoral and luckily Denys took

to stalking and enjoyed it as much as I did. We never went out together, but stalked on different beats. The thrill of a successful shot, after a long wet crawl through the heather was an exceptional pleasure. Having shot my first stag in my teens and my last in my seventies, I believe that I have terminated the lives of around 350 stags which needed to be culled. One evening while staying at the Castle, we were sitting in the drawing room with Princess Margaret. 'How is your book getting on', she asked Denys. 'It's nearly finished' he replied, 'but I desperately need a title'. At which point a voice behind us said: 'And I cannot think of a reason for giving you one'. The Queen had entered the room unobserved: this was an example of her quick repartee.

As well as crossing the Scottish border annually, we crossed many others as well, including the small country of Sikkim, where we were asked if we could be guardians to the two young grandsons of the Maharajah, who were due to go to Harrow when their prep school days ended. We gladly agreed: they were roughly the same age as our two girls and this increased the family to six. When they arrived we had to give them guidance on Western habits and etiquette. We found them somewhat out of touch with so called civilisation and we even had to teach them how to use the lavatory, they having been used to the local Indian arrangements They returned to Sikkim for the long summer holidays but stayed with us for the Christmas and Easter holidays.

The eldest boy, Tenzing was sadly killed in a car crash when he was only twenty-six years-old. The younger brother, Wanchuk was enthroned as the token 13th King of Sikkim after the death of his father from cancer in 1982, but was powerless because his kingdom had been subsumed into the Indian sub-continent by Indira

Tenzing and Wanchuk Namgyal

Ghandi. He was a very devout Buddhist and had responsibility for religious matters. He was a really nice man and was inclined to disappear on three-year long meditations living in a cave in the mountains. After they had been with us for some time, they asked if they could call me Mummy. I thought this might be rather confusing, so we settled on Auntie. Years later, when I was a Lady-in-Waiting to Queen Elizabeth, I met the present Dalai Llama, who was full of praise for Wanchuk's spirituality and dedication.

In the real world we needed extra help with our acres, but this was not affordable, so in 1973 we took the dreaded decision to sell Uplowman, where we had been so happy. There were other dark clouds on the horizon. From the earliest days of our marriage Denys would often predict that he wouldn't make 'old bones'. In 1965 he had a heart attack and spent quite a long time in hospital. My nicotine intake doubled during that time and became even greater when he came home. He had been forbidden to smoke any more, but I still needed to and took to hiding my cigarettes inside my palm or alternatively having to visit the loo more than I normally would, for a quick drag. Towards the end of his recovery from his heart attack he sank into a very deep depression. It was an awful time and lasted for almost a year. He couldn't face seeing people, even his nearest and dearest. I vividly remember the moment his illness began to recede, when we were driving up to Scotland. At one overnight stop, after dinner, we went for a short walk and suddenly he laughed. It was a blissful sound, not heard for at least a year.

We moved house twice and we were living at Spitchwick, on the edge of Dartmoor when Denys first became very seriously ill and was again taken to hospital. One day our local doctor telephoned and asked to see me. The news was bad: Denys had lung cancer, and the growth, because of its position, was inoperable. The doctor warned me bleakly that my husband had little more than a year to live. I felt as if my world had crashed into a huge, deep black abyss. I drove home hardly seeing the road through my blurred vision as the tears rolled slowly down my cheeks. Why, I wondered, couldn't one cry elegantly. Why did one have to have red blotchy eyes, and a nose needing ceaseless blowing?

I found that the only way I could cope was to live life as we had before the blow struck, at least as far as it was humanly possible. We were four or five hours driving time from either of our families and I wanted to move closer to London. Money was limited and finding a suitable property was difficult. We looked at various houses to rent but they were all much too expensive. At this stage Denys was comparatively well and he insisted that I should go as usual in October to Balmoral. Dear old Mrs Mallett came in to look after him while I was away. I have related how the Queen offered us my present home in the Great Park at Windsor. It was positively the most wonderful thing to happen. The rent was within our scope, and it meant that we would be near my sister Jean, and my aunt, Queen Elizabeth.

I am everlastingly grateful to the Queen for enabling it to happen, and I have lived there longer than I have anywhere else, surrounded by the memorabilia collected during a long and happy life. Every photograph, every painting, every piece of furniture tells a story. My immediate surroundings are not in any way grand, although there is grandeur up the road. You can't see the castle from where I live, but it's good to know that it's there, over the horizon and inhabited by people who have been so kind to me.

We took possession of The Garden House in April 1981 and in my efforts to make life relatively normal I took Denys to a little cottage we had previously rented at Cap d'Antibes. Shaun Plunket, younger brother of Patrick and his wife came to stay, and I hope that it made Denys feel that life could go on and that one could still have happy moments. We had a quiet peaceful time, lay in the sun, and shopped in the local market.

Back home, Denys was admitted to the Princess Christian Hospital in Windsor so that his condition could be monitored. He slowly began to drift away. I sat with him, held his hand and kept assuring him that I was there. He would nod, without opening his eyes and then suddenly he wasn't there anymore. He died in October 1981. It was the end of thirty-one very special and loving years. But what is love and how on earth does one know whether this one person is the one you wish to spend the whole of the rest of your life with? It is a terrifyingly difficult question. But when the love arrow strikes there is only a complete certainty that it is the right and natural thing to do. Luckily I can look back on three decades of unalloyed happiness. Even after my many years of widowhood I can relive countless happy memories. Not least of these are, of course, the children. They are my pride and joy, although it is now funny to experience a role reversal in which they now look after me and try to tell me what I can and can't do, just occasionally generating a spark of rebellion.

Family is supremely important. I never knew my paternal grandparents as they died before I was born. My father had one brother and one sister who never married. So during my childhood there were no relations on my father's side of the family. But my Strathmore grandmother had ten children, so there were a great many cousins from that clan. Fortunately for me, my mother's youngest sister's eldest child, Princess Elizabeth, coincided almost exactly in age with me, my mother's youngest. It has been my greatest good fortune to have been with my cousin through her childhood years and later as Queen. We are now both old ladies, but she is an amazing person in so many ways and I am sure that history will mark her out as an exceptional sovereign.

She has led her country unerringly through several difficult periods. She is pragmatic and able to see clearly what line to take when others have been less sure. I admire her with all my heart. But she is also a human being, a mother, daughter and sister and I fully understand the hurt that must have been caused by the marriage failures of her three eldest children. I only hope the nation does too. I clearly believe that after fifty-nine years of being Sovereign, she has seldom put a foot wrong. She has always put the good of the nation first and it is reassuring to know that we will have her son and grandson following in her footsteps.

CHAPTER SIX

On Top of the World

The wild, the remote and an element of danger have always beckoned, but I never imagined that when Denys and I received an invitation to the wedding of the Crown Prince of Sikkim in the Spring of 1963 it would set off a chain of adventures which would lead to us being arrested and detained in a very nasty coup in the Himalayan kingdom of Bhutan — or that our companion in this frightening episode would be Shirley MacLaine, the American film star.

The wedding invitation was on cream coloured hand-rolled rice paper, littered with gold coats of arms and other insignia. Officially it came from the Maharaja, or King of Sikkim, but I suppose Denys' friend from his bachelor days, Her Highness, Princess Pema Yapshi-Pheunkhang, the daughter of the King who had stayed with us the previous year was really behind it. She was known as Cocoola and was married to a Tibetan whose family was descended from a Dalai Llama. The bridegroom was her brother, His Highness Gyalsay Palden Thondup Namgyal — Thondup to his friends. He was marrying as his second wife a twenty-two year old American socialite called Hope Cooke. His first wife had been a Tibetan, who had produced two sons and then died giving birth to a daughter. The two boys, who were educated in England, had become our wards back in England.

But back to that wedding invitation. We had never met

Cocoola's brother and common sense told us that to travel 5000 expensive miles to attend the marriage of a total stranger was idiocy. But would we ever get the opportunity to experience a Buddhist royal wedding ceremony in the heart of the Himalayas? Would it not be almost criminal to turn it down? So against our better judgement we accepted and mid-April found us flying to India. Denys had the foresight to get a doctor's chit identifying him as an alcoholic, so that in 'dry' Bombay we might be able to buy some booze. We had stopovers in Calcutta, Delhi and Agra and were lucky enough to see the Taj Mahal, the world's greatest monument to love, by full moonlight. The white marble mausoleum, built by the Emperor Shah Jehan to contain the tomb of his favourite wife, seemed to float in the silver light and it was a thousand times more beautiful than I had ever dreamt.

The next lap, by an internal flight, was to Bagdogra, over the seemingly endless dry brown plains of India. We touched down at the very foot of the Himalayas and on disembarking were presented with the first of many white silk scarves, the gift of which ascribed to the recipient the blessings of long life and purity. The polite and correct response was to return the scarf to the donor, but nobody told us that and we returned home with a trunk load of them. Still, a scarf is always useful especially one with special properties. The electrifying drive, as passengers in a Sikkim version of a jeep, to the capital Gangtok was mostly through thick jungle but with hairpin bends and sheer drops. We frequently met Indian army convoys, the lorries driven by Sikhs with total abandon and disregard for what might be coming in the opposite direction. There were regular check points at which every conceivable scrap of information contained in our passports was painstakingly copied by hand.

But at last the jungle thinned and climbing over two thousand feet we were enchanted to glimpse the first houses of Gangtok clinging to the precipitous slopes, the curved blue and green roofs shining in the sun. We went straight to the guest house which came complete with an imposing Sikkimese servant whose long hair was braided round his head. After dinner that evening our friend Cocoola called in with her brother, the bridegroom. He was charming, shy and serious and came bearing the gifts of hard liquor, pouring every kind of drink down our throats, which after 'dry' India was convivially therapeutic.

The next morning we were escorted to the palace to pay our respects to the King. It was small — as palaces of my acquaintance go — and reminded me of a Scottish shooting lodge but with brilliantly covered carvings on the facade. I was bringing a message of good wishes from our Queen to their King, who met us on the doorstep. He was a tiny man, but somehow impressive and he led us into a reception room furnished with heavily brocaded sofas and chairs, the sort of thing you might have found in a five star French hotel in the days of the *belle époque*. The only thing missing were the potted palms. We sat rather nervously on the edge of our chairs and having conveyed my loyal greetings, I made some of polite conversation. Then suddenly the King said: 'Would you like to see my paintings?' I imagined a collection of Old Master works, like those which decorated the interiors of Buckingham Palace and Windsor Castle, but he led us to a small room covered floor to ceiling with strange, brightly coloured representations of mountains. They were without light or shade, or perspective. Rainbow shapes, whorls, circles and intricate patterns flared across the skies and His Majesty explained that these were symbols of the spirits, which he could see, but which — and he was very apologetic about this — we couldn't!

The dominant painting was of an immense snow capped mountain, with an awe inspiring figure bestriding the peak. This, the King explained, in quite matter of fact tones, was the Yeti — what we call the Abominable Snow Man — which always visited him on the 29th of every month. Sometimes this visitation took the form of a wild animal, but when the Yeti was in a good mood it wore golden armour.

We struggled to say the right thing, but mercifully, on that bizarre note he ushered us out of his very own National Gallery. Cocoola told us that the Yeti was intensely real to the people of Sikkim. Part spirit, part beast, it made a strange whistling noise which she imitated. Evidence of its existence was to be found in the high pastures where the bodies of yaks could be found; their necks twisted round and their huge horns embedded in the ground. Yaks are big animals and this was something that no human being could do. We spent a couple of days sightseeing, and we were later shown the chapel in the palace garden, where the Dalai Lama took refuge when he escaped from Tibet over the Nathu La pass, away from the invading Chinese.

However, it soon began to dawn on us that chaos loomed over the wedding arrangements. A large contingent of ambassadors was due from Delhi, plus an equally large number of Indian Maharajahs and a crowd of the bride's American relations. But there was no one, apart from the immediate Sikkimese royal family capable of organising anything like a royal wedding. My only experience of such an event had been that of Princess

Elizabeth, sixteen years earlier, and then my role had been solely decorative. George VI had solved his guest accommodation problem by putting most of them up in Claridges and picking up the bill, but in faraway Sikkim it was all hands to the pumps as they say.

We soon set ourselves to work, ferrying bed clothes, curtains, carpets, cushions, towels, soap, champagne, whisky, flowers, even copious supplies of disinfectant to a village of bamboo huts called bashas where the ambassadors and the American VIPs were to stay. The Maharajahs were to be installed for the duration in an ugly newly built block of flats, appropriately called Elephant Mansions. We organised a press reception with lots of liquor and a rather more restrained Corps Diplomatique reception to appease the ambassadors who were complaining because insufficient attention was being paid to them.

We assumed the roles of Master of the Royal Household, Equerries, Ladies-in-Waiting and Footmen. Drawing on my memories of grand affairs at Buckingham Palace and Windsor Castle we ensured that table cloths were cleaned and ironed, drew up seating plans; arranged the flowers, polished and counted the glasses and plates; kept pork away from the Muslims and the strong stuff from the drunks. We dished out birds nest soup, sea slugs, tripe, octopi and a great many other things the ingredients of which we were only too happy to be ignorant about. And all this gluttony was before the wedding day itself.

The ceremony itself was pure theatre, the curtain rising on a scene of great splendour. I was in my most elegant Ascot outfit, and Denys wore a tail coat and top hat. The American women looked as if they had stepped straight out of a Hollywood movie:

Central Casting would have been proud. But the Sikkimese and Indian women outshone us westerners, shimmering in saris of brocade, gold and silver lame, floating chiffon and gleaming satin. Top hats mixed with turbans and fezzes and the Sikkimese royal family resembled jewelled Fabergé ornaments. The King and the bridegroom were in stiff, brocaded gold coats, and the bride was in white, with a silver lamé cloak, her dark hair piled high. The jewellery which decorated all these people must have been priceless, but the congregation also included many poor Tibetan refugees who had settled in Sikkim.

The chapel was illuminated by hundreds of little butter fuelled lamps. The bride and bridegroom sat cross legged on a high dais and to put the demons to flight a Llama band blew trumpet fanfares louder than any Joshua ever knew. Important parts were played by 'the Man of the Earth Serpent Year' followed by 'the Boy of the Water Dragon Year' and 'the Lady of the Iron Horse Year', to mention just three invocations of divine symbolism. There were lots of prayers and the bride lit the sacred lamp before the altar of the Lord Buddha. Heaven knows what the American guests made of it all, and, as I overheard one confused blonde remark: 'We just don't do it this way on Rhode Island'.

The palace gardens were festooned with coloured lights draped from tree to tree. One very large tree was unadorned and we were warned not to go too close, because the spirit of an old man lived there and did not wish to be disturbed. Regardless of this injunction one of the King's grandsons, about ten-years-old, kicked the trunk, saying that he didn't believe in all that rubbish. We learned the next morning that his kicking leg was so badly swollen that he couldn't walk. The spirit of the old man had obviously been seriously discomfited. The palace doctor was baffled, but then the Buddhist version of a witch doctor was summoned to do his stuff; cast a spell and lo and behold the princeling rose from his bed and walked. Were we, I pondered, in a land of miracles?

The religious ceremony at last over, four full days of partying began. A smart Bombay band had been imported and played up to the minute European rock and roll. It was strange to see the Sikkimese and the Tibetans gyrating away like mad, the girls as graceful as reeds. Even the little old King took to the floor. The kilted palace guard was on duty, and like all good mountain men they had a pipe band. Someone suggested, certainly not me, that an exhibition Eightsome reel should be performed. The Gangtok school mistress, Martha Hamilton, a Scotswoman far from home and I were the only guests who knew how to dance it, but all I can say is that it was nothing like the Ghillies ball at Balmoral. The pipers never quite achieved the right time, and the gentlemen participants were all Indian generals who had taken full advantage of the liberal liquid refreshments. Total chaos ensued and I hoped that the audience thought we were a comedy turn. My partner was a towering Sikh and we made a right spectacle of ourselves. I was thankful that no other Scots were present to witness my disgrace. Sadly, despite a wedding heavy with religion and mysticism Thondup and his wife divorced in 1980, and although he did his best, he also had a rough ride as King. By the early 1970s there were rumblings in the political rank and file, demanding the removal of the country's ancient monarchy and the establishment of a more democratic government. I suppose it was inevitable, but in 1975 Sikkim became the twenty-second state in the Indian Union and the authority of its King was removed. Thondup died a heartbroken and lonely man.

But that was all in the then unknown future, and before we left we were introduced to the Prime Minister of Bhutan, Jigme Djorgi, who made a tentative suggestion that the following year we might visit his country. It was next door to Sikkim and not long before had been an enclosed sort of Shangri-la; the last place on the roof of the world, isolated and only possible for strangers to enter as guests of either the King or the Prime Minister.

Jigme Djorgi was quite enthusiastic, but it was a fateful encounter. Over the next twelve months plans went ahead for our Bhutan exploration, the correspondence being conducted directly with the Prime Minister. The arrangements were progressing well, but one morning, sitting having breakfast in our dining room in Devon, Denys picked up *The Times* and was horrified to read a report that Jigme Djorgi had been assassinated. That very morning we had received a letter from him saying he was looking forward to welcoming us to Bhutan. Very spooky. We assumed that our trip would now be impossible, but after a gap of a few weeks we received a signal from the new Prime Minister, Lhendup Djorgi that it could go ahead. Under the hereditary system in Bhutan he had succeeded his murdered brother in office.

We flew to Calcutta and spent two nights with a married couple of our acquaintance. They had a large house and garden, and a swimming pool that appeared to be filled with warm green soup. Perhaps our hosts were suffering from a lack of chlorine. Our next destination was once again Sikkim, for a trek into the high western country, which started in the autumn. Since our wedding visit the old King had died and Thondup had succeeded him. By coincidence he was flying in from Zurich and met us in the VIP lounge at Calcutta airport. On the way to the airport, we passed a huge advertisement announcing in three feet high scarlet letters: 'Blood, urine, sputum and pus examined here' – a charming thought to carry with us.

Together with our host we then emplaned for the flight to Bagdogra in the foothills of the Himalayas. After a few ceremonies we set off in Thondup's Mercedes sports car for the palace escorted by Jeep load of Sikkim guardsmen. The police commissioner led the cavalcade, waving a red flag to warn all other drivers off the road. At each Sikkimese village along the way Thondup's procession stopped for ceremonies of welcome. At each village we were garlanded with marigolds and even more white scarves.

That night we were put up at the palace. We had an en-suite bathroom, which was a great luxury. Denys decided that his hair needed attention and having forgotten to pack his Mr Trumper's hair lotion, in desperation he used my anti-perspirant lotion to smooth his locks. At first the results were quite pleasing, but after a while it set like concrete and he looked like something out of Madame Tussauds. We had dinner at little individual tables and were given chopsticks. Our hopelessness in using them reduced the waiting Sikkimise servants to giggles.

Our trek at last started. We drove to a small guest house where the road stopped. It was pouring with rain and the windscreen wipers didn't work – it got dark and we got lost. Eventually we arrived, quite late in the evening. We ate something out of a tin and crept into our sleeping bags, only to be woken by the arrival of some Indian soldiers, who we discovered had swiped our bottle of whisky; Denys was not pleased. After some porters were found to carry our tents and provisions, which included a live goat, we set off on foot. We soon came upon a small Gumpa – a chapel, where we were greeted by a venerable monk, who led us in and seated us, offering us dirty glasses of what looked like water.

As old crone appeared and pointing at our glasses, she whirled around, laughing madly and pretending to be drunk. A sip confirmed that it would be safer to abstain. That night was spent at Yoksam, a tiny community, where the first King of Sikkim had been crowned. The village headman came to meet us and invite us to his house for the evening. It was dark when we got there and we came to a small room filled with people. In the flickering light we could just make out the ochre-robed figure of the village monk in the corner. We were given Chanf to drink, which is made from millet seed. We drank from hollowed out bamboo cups, which were filled up from an old black kettle. The women started to dance and invited me to join them – it was a memorable evening.

We spent a total of four nights camping, the last at 14,000 feet. Denys began to feel ill with mountain sickness – luckily I was all right and decided to walk on up to 15,000 feet where there were some rows of prayer flags. The view was spell-binding. We had achieved our objective and had walked in the region of 70 miles in four days.

After our return, we were glad of a few days of complete idleness in the palace at Gangtok. There were endless lunch and dinner parties and it soon became clear that there was some difficulty in getting us passes for Bhutan. It also appeared that we were becoming unpopular with the Indian officials in Gangtok. Denys was also accused, falsely, of trying to infiltrate the almost non-existent mining operations in the country, all because of some conversation he had had about his uranium expedition to Tanzania in the copper belt. Eventually our passes arrived and at last on 8 November we started the long-awaited expedition to Bhutan, which unbeknown to us, was on the brink of another plot-ridden political crisis. Thondup lent us one of his ADCs, a good natured young man whose job it was to ease us along the way. He was very useful since we did not speak a word of Sikkimese or Hindi.

The first lap of our journey took ten hours, instead of half that time that had been optimistically forecast, because of a broken bridge. When at last we arrived at the guest house at Phuntsoling we were a bit shaken to find that this was where our host, Jigme Dorgi, had been assassinated. The next morning we transferred from the royal Jeep to another vehicle with a local driver. It was a fascinating drive with breathtaking views but the roads were appalling and under repair every inch of the way. Sometimes it was necessary to shut one's eyes and involuntarily hit the floor in a braking fashion. Our driver was a carefree fellow who put his foot down whenever the opportunity occurred, regardless of the thousand foot drop on one side of the road.

After another nine and a half hours of bone shaking travel our driver suddenly braked to a halt. It was dusk, but we could make out a large vehicle parked by the side of the road. It was our welcoming party, a charming girl who introduced herself as Mary Macdonald, the Prime Minister's social secretary. She was of Scottish, Tibetan, and Indian blood, and related to the celebrated Macdonald family who for generations owned the Himalayan Hotel in Kalimpong, once part of Bhutan but now in the present

Indian state of West Bengal. She was accompanied by an Indian gentleman exquisitely dressed in a pearl grey suit, topped off with a Homburg hat in the style favoured by King Edward VII. He said he was the Quartermaster General, i/c guest houses, and offered us sweet tea and biscuits.

We slept that night in a house in Paro. We now entered a period of considerable confusion. It was pointless to plan ahead as our future movements depended on the arrival of our host, the Prime Minister, and there was no sign of him. It was then arbitrarily decided by our minders to move us to Thimbu. Whatever she had heard on the grapevine at the royal guest house there made Mary Macdonald jittery and so we began to feel jittery too. Nobody wanted to take responsibility for us. Mary did not trust the servants, but refused to explain why. Perhaps she knew something we didn't. The Quartermaster General — he of the Homburg hat — said that all his colleagues had gone off to Kalimpong to meet the Prime Minister who was due to attend a very important ceremony at a place called Har where every year the Oracle spoke a prophecy for the fortunes of all in the coming year. The ceremony was of great religious and political importance.

The next day, to pass the time and to allay our growing disquiet, we were taken to a monastery, riding there on small donkeys with two young attendants called Jo and Pemba, who enlivened our two hour climb by blowing on llama horns and clashing cymbals. In other circumstances it might have been fun, but I could not rid myself of the feeling of being in a Bhutanese limbo, with sinister undertones. We were now told that the Prime Minister was definitely not going to Har. He had received intelligence reports of a plot to shoot him during the ceremony and therefore he was not coming to see us either. A senior army officer was, however, on his way with orders. 'Curiouser and curiouser', as Alice in Wonderland said.

The next morning a Brigadier did indeed turn up and organised the mules and ponies for our expedition to Har. We formed an extraordinary procession, a long straggling four footed line, with bells jingling and the Bhutanese escort giving out strange, high pitched yells. There was a mixed assortment of tack. Our saddles were made of wood and the stirrups were of fixed length, which made riding incredibly uncomfortable. Some of the animals had only one rein and none of them had bits, which made steering problematical. The horses chose in which order we were to ride and it was useless to argue with them. It was actually a wonderful ride. We climbed slowly to the top of the immediate mountain. We crossed over grassland with scattered pines and birches and then deeper into thicker forest. We had been late in starting the expedition and so found darkness creeping up on us. The moon was full and it cast silver streaks of light through the black trunks of the pines. The going was very rough and so we decided to dismount and walk the last few miles in complete darkness until at last we came upon the faint lights of the encampment at Har.

Our journey had taken eight hours and we were stiff and weary. On our way we had encountered a small party travelling in the opposite direction. It turned out to be the widow of the murdered Prime Minister. She was enraged that the Oracle ceremony was going ahead so soon after his death. 'First they shoot him and now they do this — it's so hypocritical', she said angrily, before retreating down the slope. Har had been a personal estate of the

Djorgi family and they had voluntarily given it over to the military. We were put up in the Brigadier's personal quarters and were woken early the next morning to prepare for the long ride to the site of the ceremony. We were both lent some local clothing, which in my case consisted of a long brocade dress, worn over a silk shirt. Denys was given a very smart black brocade coat which was knee length and under this he insisted on wearing grey flannel trousers. It was apparently unthinkable that a Bhutanese gentleman would be seen in public without a sword. Denys was thus accoutred with an enormously long weapon, which when he was astride a pony, clanked ominously against his leg.

We finally set out in a small procession, riding up a grassy valley with a little stream running through it. There were stops at various moments on the way at which small canons would be approached warily by a helmeted warrior carrying a lighted taper. Having lit the fuse, he ran like hell to take cover, before the expected explosion occurred. It was a deliciously medieval sight. At last, after riding for over two hours, we came to the natural end of the valley which spread out into a wide open expanse, filled with a bustling noisy crowd. There was no one in European clothes. Instead, they were clad in a colourful mixture of brocade dresses and fur hats, beneath which glowed happy Mongol faces. Mixing in with all these were the ochre coloured figures of Buddhist monks. The ceremony included many things that were not at all akin to Buddhist teaching. The first was a sudden appearance of a yak, which was paraded around and garlanded with golden marigolds. It was then taken away and slaughtered (not very Buddhist). Later a group of village elders danced a in a slow circle, brandishing their swords.

The main object of the whole festival was a pronouncement by the Oracle, which was deemed to foretell what the coming year would bring. To assist his pronouncement, the Oracle was generously supplied with liquor from dawn onwards, with the purpose of making him so inebriated that he could not speak his own words, but only those of the God who presided over the whole festival. An altar had been built and little butter lamps twinkled around it. Then suddenly the Oracle appeared. He wore a crimson garment and a spiky crimson hat. He started dancing around the altar, weaving a drunken circle. Then he got angry. He was shouting and started destroying the altar. The crowd was hushed. One felt the tension. They all needed a good omen. The Oracle disappeared and there was total silence. Then he suddenly reappeared. He looked different and his anger was gone. He danced again, but more soberly and then he spoke a few words, which were of course incomprehensible to us, but apparently it was deemed sufficient to keep the crowd satisfied.

It hardly seemed possible that we had witnessed an ancient ceremony deep in the Himalayas in a small kingdom with an absolute monarch. We later discovered that the Oracle had denounced the modernisation of the country and had demanded that more attention be paid to the Buddhist religion. The people were happy with these sentiments and were just glad that there had not been a prophesy of foreboding as there had been the previous year — the year in which the Prime Minister had been assassinated.

The whole episode was surreal. Was this, I wondered, truly representative of mid twentieth century Bhutan. Finally we climbed back on to our wooden saddles and bumped our weary way back to the Har guest house where we heard the news that Shirley MacLaine, who was also exploring in Bhutan as a guest of the Prime Minister, was about to arrive in Paro. We rode back there the next day, through driving snow, and found Shirley waiting for us in the guest house with another of the Prime Minister's aides called Bhalla. We soon made friends. Shirley turned out to be nice and easy and not the least bit like I imagined a film star to be. We were due to leave Bhutan within the next couple of days. Everything seemed to be going to plan, but then we noticed that Mary Macdonald and Bhalla were spending a great deal of time whispering in corners and looking tense. We began to have our first inklings of serious trouble ahead when they suggested that we should make straight for the frontier with India.

There had been a plot to oust the new Prime Minister, our host, and all the pro Djorgi factions were under suspicion, if not lock and key. The Prime Minister was bitterly resented by the old guard religious diehards, because of his attempts to open up the country to the west, and drag it into the twentieth century. He was thought by his opponents to be too powerful. It occurred to me that we were representatives of this opening up process. Mary told us that our Quartermaster friend had been arrested, together with several other officials in the Prime Minister's entourage, including Shirley's other aide Larry; and that the two most senior officers in the army had fled across the border with their wives and children. Mary and Bhalla were making remarks like: 'The Quartermaster will only last three days under torture'. We began to learn something of the sinister side of Bhutanese life and Mary told us bedtime stories of how women condemned of witchcraft were still being punished by being stitched up in a fresh yak skin and then left out in the sun to suffocate as the skin contracted. There was also a savage army routine which involved offenders being made to run round the parade ground with large stones attached to their genitalia. Aldershot at its most brutal was never like that!

The situation was unnerving. We were in remote and unknown territory and knew no one to turn to for advice. Bhutan was an absolute monarchy, with a royal family who were all at odds with each other. They were like something out of *The Prisoner of Zenda* and we could envisage no help from that quarter. We wanted to send a message to Sikkim so that transport would meet us at the border to take us back to Gangtok, but this plan stalled because any messages to the outside world had to be countersigned by the King's brother which was impossible to achieve. We were cut off and apart from poor Mary and Bhalla, who were far more at risk than us, we were friendless. We decided to hot foot it to the frontier at Phuntsoling and then cross into India. As we were leaving, Mary was slipped a letter. It was from Larry, saying that the crisis was deepening and that the situation was becoming increasingly dangerous. Several more people had been arrested.

Our group left Paro at crack of dawn squashed into two small Jeeps with inadequate suspension systems. It was another nightmare journey of hairpin bends and sheer drops, made even more frightening by the road blocks manned by surly gun toting Bhutanese soldiers who were very reluctant to let us through. It was a ten hour drive, but at Phuntsoling we decided to press on and get the hell out of Bhutan that very evening, to avoid the arrest of Mary and Bhalla, which, in our fraught state of mind, seemed a strong possibility.

A minor official told us we couldn't cross the frontier without exit permits, but then Denys located the only senior officer left on station and spun him a story that we had just received news that we were urgently required in Sikkim. The officer said he would have to refer the request up the line, and that if we returned to the guest house and had something to eat the permits would be issued before we had finished out meal. We could barely get through a mouthful, and Shirley was convinced that the food was poisoned. Then we heard the sound of barked orders and the crunch of marching feet outside the door. This certainly did not betoken the delivery of our permits, and we looked out of the window to see a troop of soldiers surrounding the house, with their rifles pointing inwards at the windows and doors. We were conclusively under house arrest.

The next fright was a banging on the door. It was yet another jobsworth, but miraculously with our exit permits, minus one. Bhalla was to be left behind, under detention, to face possible torture and execution. We couldn't desert him, and our first ploy was to try and disguise him as one of our Bhutanese drivers, who we stripped of his clothes despite his vociferous protests. We were all geared up to leave, but after checking, with a last look through the window, Bhalla saw that the officer at the gate was someone he knew and was bound to recognise him. Our first plan was obviously doomed to failure, so then we decided that our only chance was to conceal him under the pile of luggage in the back of our Jeep. Luck seemed to be with us and after several nail biting minutes we were waved on by the guard and drove on into the night. But some distance on we saw bright lights and a barrier across the road: it was a 'Checkpoint Charlie'. In the illuminations we could detect a platoon of soldiers, although they couldn't see us as we were still in an unlit area. We switched our lights off and called a crisis conference. If Bhalla was found it would be very dangerous for us, and rather than cause a diplomatic incident we turned round in the direction of the guest house. At a very black spot on the road we stopped and told Bhalla to run for India, which was only two miles away. We would wait for a while and then pick him up on the Indian side.

He disappeared into the dark and we returned to the guest house, pretending to have left something vital behind. But we soon became acutely aware that the Chief Liaison Officer knew that Bhalla had escaped. The soldiers were furiously searching for him and in a rage the CLO shouted that he would not let any of us go until he had his man. By now it was after midnight and we sat around hoping that Bhalla would have had time to reach Indian territory. Despite the CLO's protests we were allowed to leave, but as we approached the checkpoint we met an army vehicle coming in the opposite direction, and could clearly see the hunched figure of Bhalla sitting in the back under guard.

We jammed on our brakes; turned and followed. When the military vehicle stopped we tumbled out and ran towards Bhalla. He was handcuffed and had been badly beaten up. We learnt later that he had managed to get within a few yards of the border and then came upon a Jeep which he thought was ours. It was a disastrous misjudgement. It was a Bhutanese army vehicle and he was immediately taken prisoner and knocked about. Our plan was now in tatters and we had no choice but to swing around and follow the army Jeep down to the CLO's office. We threw our weight around, such as it was, and managed to get the handcuffs off Bhalla. By now the CLO was raging. He tore up our exit permits and placed us under arrest, forbidden to leave the country until the pleasure of His Bhutanese Majesty was known. In desperation I invoked the name of the Queen of England, shouting that she was my first cousin, while Shirley declaimed that she was a famous American actress, and that the whole firmament of Hollywood would rise up in protest, led by her brother Warren Beatty, at the way she was being treated.

But it was no good. The names of Queen Elizabeth II, Warner Brothers and MGM failed to impress our captors. We then demanded a telephone to speak to Thondup in Gangtok but were told that the lines were down. We were, however, surprisingly taken to an office near the checkpoint where there was an antiquated radio telephone. We spent two and a half hours trying to get through to Sikkim, but it was in the middle of the night and all the exchanges appeared shut down. We relayed messages through a signal's officer to the Bhutanese higher command, and eventually received the frightening reply that Mary Macdonald and Bhalla were to be kept prisoner, and that there was no chance of us leaving the country. Denys and I then stage-managed a row with the CLO outside the office, as cover for Mary while she tried to get through to somebody — anybody — to alert them to our predicament. But after only a few minutes of Mary's angry telephonic shouting, the CLO realised what was going on and rushed into the radio telephone room to rip out the connections.

We were then ordered to return to the guest house. Mary and Bhalla were to be taken away, to God knows what. We could not permit this and surrounding them managed somehow to smuggle them inside. We dragged all the mattresses off the beds and laid them side by side in the main room, placing Mary and Bhalla in the middle. Some soldiers burst in during what was left of the night, bent on removing Mary and Bhalla from our protection, but seeing us all huddled close together gave up and went away. Early next morning we were ordered back into the CLO's office and found that suddenly everything had changed. He actually managed a smile. Word had come from the King personally that we were ALL to be allowed to leave. We didn't wait. We headed for Sikkim, while Shirley, Bhalla and Mary made for Calcutta, where Shirley was devoured by a hungry press. Thus ended a dramatic episode, bit it didn't put me off exploring. I have to add that Bhutan is now a democracy under a twenty-eight-years-old King, the world's youngest monarch. In 2006 the magazine *Business Week* rated it the happiest country in Asia. What a difference the passing of the years make.

CHAPTER SEVEN

African Adventure

Africa had cast its spell over me from the very moment I landed at Nairobi airport in the winter of 1955. Denys, who was researching a book about locust control, had gone ahead of me by at least a month as it was difficult for European women to enter many of the places he wanted to visit, such as Somalia. I hitched a lift in a light plane to the locust control camp, hoping to rendezvous with my husband, but sweethearts and wives were frowned upon in its all-male environment, so I was packed off back to Nairobi, where I then embarked on a lone woman tour to stay with anyone who would have me. I ended up on a farm on the slopes of Mount Kilimanjaro and was filled with a burning desire to scale its magical peak. It is an ambition as yet unfulfilled, and I fear will remain so.

I loved the fact that the mountain had been given by Queen Victoria to Prince Friedrich of Prussia when he married her daughter, Vicky, the Princess Royal, in 1858. As a result the mountain became part of German Tanganyika and the mapmakers had to draw a little bubble in the straight line of the frontier between British Kenya and Tanganyika. The imperial couple reigned briefly as German Emperor and Empress; Fritz, as he was known being seriously ill and dying just three months after his accession. They had strong liberal and Anglophile leanings, completely at variance with their eldest son, 'Kaiser Bill', who took Germany into the First World War. It is a simplistic view, but I like to think that there would have been no First World War; and subsequently no Hitler, and no Second World War if Fritz had lived.

But I digress. Eventually I was scooped up by some friends of Denys' cousin, Shaun Plunket; a friendship formed while he was doing a stint in Kenya with the British army. Peter and Susie Marrian had a coffee farm set beneath the Aberdare Mountains and I had arrived to experience the Mau Mau uprising at its height. The insurgents were nearly all Kikuyu, a tribe living between the farm and Nairobi, ninety miles away. They were actually more civilised than many of the other tribes, but some were committed to the savagery of the Mau Mau rebellion. In fact they murdered more of their own people than white settlers, although the atrocities involving Europeans made the biggest headlines.

One of their tricks was to terrorise the house servants so as to gain access to the houses of whites. At meal times on the farm, we sat with a gun each beside our plates and the house boy was locked into the room with us, using a hatch to receive food from the kitchen. All the farm workers and most of the house staff were Kikuyu and it was difficult to know whom to trust. Our soldiers had to camouflage themselves and hide for days in the forest while trying to locate Mau Mau camps, but more soldiers were killed by marauding rhino than by the Mau Mau. I didn't, however, let the Mau Mau stop me riding every morning, often exploring areas known to be dangerous. I was being foolhardy, but I found this gun toting expeditions exciting and would often come across buffalo and rhinos. The rhinos fascinated me, and occasionally I'd follow one, believing that if it charged I could easily out gallop it. Later I discovered that when a rhino charges it can travel faster than a Derby winner.

119

We would sometimes drive up into the forest, hoping to see a few Rhino, although this was frowned on by the security services, as the whole Aberdare region was a Mau Mau fiefdom. From the forest boundary one could walk to Treetops, an observation point built in a giant fig tree and overlooking a water hole frequented by animals. It was there, in 1952, that Princess Elizabeth, at the start of a Commonwealth tour, became Queen. She was filming wild life when her father, King George VI, died in his sleep at Sandringham, three thousand miles away. While she was there two water buck had a fight, and one was fatally wounded. There is a Kikuyu legend that when two water buck meet in combat and one dies, this signals the death of a great chief. How strange that that came true that night. Regrettably, Treetops was torched by the Mau Mau, but it was rebuilt on a much larger scale on the same site. The Queen made a return visit there in 1983.

Back in 1952, I sent a letter of condolence to the new Queen, and six days after she succeeded to the throne she replied, saying that I had 'struck the nail on the head' by saying that it must have been 'agony' to be away when 'Papa died', and adding: 'It really was ghastly; the feeling that I was unable to help or comfort Mummy or Margaret, and that there was nothing one could do at all'. He had died 'so suddenly', leaving her stunned, shocked and disbelieving. She thanked me for my letter, and said, touchingly: 'Letters are such a comfort, and every one of them gives me further courage to go on'.

A year or two later Denys went alone to Zambia, gathering information for a new book. It was there that he met Jolyon Halse, who later moved to Kenya with his wife Stafford. They became very great friends, and as he was a freelance geologist, he was fully

Sikkim, March 1963

Me in the Himalayas in Sikkim

Denys in Sikkim

Sikkim, March 1963

Tibetan refugee camp - Princess Cocoola in Sikkim

Victor Whitworth and Princess Cocoola at the Palace in Sikkim

Sikkim, March 1963

Thondup and Hope before their wedding

Princess Coola and Sikkimise guards

Bhutan, 1964

Denys and me in the Himalayas at 14,000 ft

Ha Festival in Honour of the God of War

Bhutan, 1964

Mary Macdonald, me and Ming

Sikkimese New Year – Princess Cocoola and me in Sikkimese dress

Stafford Halse and me at Lake Rudolph, Kenya, 1974

Mount Kulal, Kenya. Stafford Halse, me and Jolyon Halse

1989. Me with two Thompson's gazelle. *Risasi moja* is Swahili for 'one bullet'

With my children, Annabel, Simon, Victoria and Michael at Garden House, Windsor

The Royal Household, Clarence House, 1979, with Queen Elizabeth

equipped for every possible kind of safari. It became a passport for us to see many parts of the country, which would have been impossible for the ordinary tourist. One time, sitting in the Halse's garden in Kenya, we began planning a safari to the far north of the country. We had long wanted to explore the remoter regions of the Northern Frontier District, the wildest and most exciting part of Kenya, hoping to circumnavigate Lake Rudolf, now called Lake Turkana. This was an over ambitious plan as we had, at that stage, no idea about the driving conditions or the time that such a trip would take. If we wished to go right round the lake, it would, as a geographical necessity, mean entering Ethiopia, where the river Omo would have to be crossed. I had a wonderful idea that we should get Lever Brothers to script a commercial showing us washing our smalls in the river Omo with Omo washing powder!

As luck would have it, that following summer we were delighted to be invited to a dinner at Windsor Castle, in honour of Emperor Haile Selassie, Emperor of Ethiopia. He was over to attend the Garter Service in St George's Chapel, having in 1954 been made a Knight of the Order, Britain's oldest order of chivalry. The Emperor would only admit to speaking French, so the Queen placed me beside him, as she knew that I would be able to converse reasonably well in that language. It seemed strange to be seated in one of the oldest inhabited British castles, talking French to an African Emperor. He, of course, sat on the Queen's right, and I was able to study him covertly until it came to my turn to talk to him. He was small and spare, with the finely honed features of the Nilotic people. I took the chance to ask him if we would be allowed to cross into his country, so as to reach Lake Rudolf in Kenya, the far northern end of which cuts into Ethiopia. He indicated that this would be possible, with the brief reply: '*Mais oui, naturellement*' and although I never received a personally signed pass. I suppose, in the circumstances, he couldn't say '*Non*'.

After all, the Queen was entertaining not only himself and many members of his family, but also his large retinue. It was Royal Ascot week and the Queen was hosting her usual Ascot house party. Little did we know then of the Emperor's tragic future. In 1974, the year after we met, he was deposed, spending the last months of his life as a prisoner. Many members of his family were executed, but when he died in 1975 the official government version of his end was that he suffered respiratory failure following complications after routine surgery. Suspicions about the cause of his death remain and supporters believe he was assassinated. In 1992 his bones were found under a concrete slab in the grounds of his palace and reports suggested that they were discovered beneath a latrine. His Garter banner, which during his lifetime hung in St George's Chapel, was returned by the Queen to the surviving members of his family.

We returned to Kenya in the early spring of 1974 and began serious planning. It would be advisable to have two vehicles in case of disaster. The aim was to circumnavigate Lake Rudolf, the world's largest permanent desert lake, named in 1888 in honour of Crown Prince Rudolf of Austria by an Austrian explorer, Count Samuel Teleki de Szek, who was the first European to have visited the lake, which after Kenyan independence was renamed Lake Turkana after the region's predominant tribe. At last D-Day arrived. Jolyon and Stafford Halse, and Denys and I, set off from Nairobi on 7 February 1974, driving north through Nyeri and on over the shoulder of Mount Kenya, and then down towards Isiolo and the flat plains which stretch endlessly towards the horizon. We made camp the first night by the banks of the Uso Nyro and for the first time heard the roar of lions, the most exciting noise imaginable.

Soon after leaving our camp at first light, we caught sight of the wonderfully shaped Mount Ololokwe rising with incredible suddenness from the desert plain, its sides steep and cliff like and its top completely flat, which reminded me of Sir Arthur Conan Doyle's *The Lost World*, the sort of place where one can imagine that prehistoric beasts might still roam. Further on, we came to Marsabit, another mountain rising alone out of the desert, tree covered, and home to herds of elephants. The great Ahmed, Kenya's largest elephant lived there, whose long tusks swept the ground, a valuable feature which put him constantly at risk from ivory traders and he had his own platoon of Askaris to guard him from potential poachers.

We made camp that night on a horrible, windswept plain. We hardly slept and left very early, with no other vehicles to be seen. We were now to cross the Chalbi desert and passed a noisy and colourful meeting place, for what I think was the Rendille tribe. There were a hundred of them with their camels, and it was a great treat to have seen them. Later we reached a small oasis of tall reeds, and decided to stop and have a look. We had with us our guide, armed only with a spear. We were walking in the grove when suddenly some atavistic instinct brought on a sense of danger. Then I saw the glint of metal and dark faces hiding in the reeds. It was the Shifta and their guns were pointing directly at us. It was not a good idea to run, and so with our hearts in our mouths we assumed nonchalance and sauntered back to our vehicles. The Shifta could have finished us off and stripped us of our belongings. Why they didn't I'll never know. Wild animals would have completed the job and we would have simply become another example of travellers who had just disappeared.

Our journey became increasingly rough as we drove over ridges of black lava. It was incredibly hot, and ridge after ridge succeeded each other as we began to despair of actually ever reaching the lake, which is about three hundred miles long. But at long last, as we crested yet another rise, we caught a glimpse of water ahead. It was the Turquoise Sea, stretching as far as the eye could see. Our first instinct when we reached the shore was to jump straight in to cool down and we waded out into the deliciously cold water. Then one of guides spotted a flotilla of two eyed lumps breaking the surface. They were crocodiles, the sight of which put a dip right out of our minds. We were told afterwards that the lake contained Africa's largest population of Nile crocodiles, 14,000 of them, and all very hungry indeed. It was a lucky escape.

Our next problem was to find a possible campsite. We saw a line of trees some distance away, but when we got nearer, to our horror, we spotted a land rover already parked there, the first vehicle we had seen for over 200 miles. We drove on regardless, and to our astonishment, found that the occupant of the camp was none other than Wilfred Thesiger, the remarkable explorer of Africa and Arabia. He was kindness himself and showed us another site a little further away, where we camped. We invited him to dinner and he told us enthralling stories of Kenya and the Empty Quarter of Southern Arabia — and also frightening ones of the murders of local missionaries by a gang of bandits known as the Shifta, mostly Somali from over the border. Wilfred Thesiger had lived with the tribal peoples of East Africa since 1968, only occasionally returning home. He was knighted in 1995 and I met him again over lunch with Queen Elizabeth at Clarence House. He was nearly blind by then, but he remembered our chance meeting so many years before.

We went off the following morning to scout out the land further north. There was a howling, hot gale and there were no visible tracks to follow, though the ground was hard and easy to drive on. At one point, Jolyon leant out of the window to point out some lion spoor. We stopped to look further, only to suddenly see two large black-maned lions lying down about twenty yards away; we re-embarked pretty fast. It now became clear that we would not succeed in our planned aim of reaching the Ethiopian border. The drive to the lake had taken far longer than anticipated, due mainly to the very slow going over the endless plains.

We rescheduled our plans and aimed instead for Mount Kulal on the eastern side of the lake. Over 7000 feet high it was split in two by a great chasm. One side had a mission station on it, while the other was largely unknown, with no track up it. We had some confusing and unclear notes made up by a British Army survey team, which included such gems as 'turn left where there are three thorn trees'. There is, of course, one thorn tree per foot of ground in Kenya. Despite such difficulties, we looked for any wheel tracks and continued to climb until darkness fell and our headlights carved columns of light into the black sky. We could no longer see what was under our wheels and had to stop.

We camped in the teeth of a howling gale: it was impossible to cook so we bedded down hungry, and with a sense of potential danger. We had seen a rhino in the headlights before we stopped and there had been signs of other animals around. We left at first light and soon came upon the ruins of a pipe-laid water supply. Sadly, with no Europeans still here, it had been not been maintained, though no doubt elephants had something to do with it. At last we reached a bare grass mound and found two wood cabins, protected from the eternal wind, looking like a Wild West film. They had been built to allow the local British administrators to escape the heat of Lake Rudolf below. We quickly made them our home and that night enjoyed a proper cooked meal. There is no pleasure to equal that of siting round a campsite at night, after a long hot day, drinking a whisky under the vast and wonderful canopy of the African sky.

In the morning we received a visit from a good-looking young warrior. He was bare-headed and was wearing only the ubiquitous piece of red cloth, and armed with a spear. He had a particularly handsome necklace, on which the Halses commented. He told them that it indicated that he had killed a man. We decided to go exploring and soon came upon a spring in the forest, where the cattle were watering. We were greeted with suspicious looks by the cattle herders, as water is such a precious commodity and intruders are unwelcome. After a bit of Swahili banter, they offered to show us the way to the summit, which we had failed to reach the day before. This was great news, as of course there were no tracks to follow.

Our guide was a splendid man with a turaco feather stuck in his curly hair. As we climbed, the trees became stunted and we were fascinated to see the tracks of lion and elephant as we climbed, which was surprising at such a great height. At last we reached the top, which was bare and grassy. Almost immediately below us was the chasm dividing the two parts of Kulal. The ground fell away into dizzying depths, where the mist swirled and one really felt that no European had set foot before. We could see swifts flying and we could hear the thrumming of their wings.

Far, far below we could see the faint blue smudge of the lake. I shall never forget that particular sight. There were other safaris, but this one has always stood out as the most exciting of them all.

Another adventure was to Petra. Years later, after Denys died, I was at Sandringham staying with the Queen, when I met Crown Prince Hassan of Jordan and his wife Sarvath, the daughter of the Foreign Minister of Pakistan. They were very nice and friendly. One traveller's tale led to another, and over dinner one evening I told Prince Hassan that I had long wanted to visit Petra, described by John William Burgon as 'a rose red city, half as old as time'. They immediately invited me to stay with them at their place in Amman, together with Lady Susan Hussey, one of the Queen's Ladies-in-Waiting, who was at Sandringham at the time of their visit.

Prince Hassan had been heir to the Hashemite kingdom of Jordan for three decades, until in 1988 his brother, King Hussein, named his own son Prince Abdullah as his heir. It must have been a great shock to him, as it was done so abruptly and so unexpectedly. Hassan and Sarvath were charming hosts, but they kept apart in the day because of the regulations for Ramadan. When we accompanied them we went everywhere in a heavily armour plated car, the doors of which weighed a ton to open or shut. Hassan and his wife were greeted enthusiastically by the villagers we met and it was obvious that they were very popular. At one time we stayed in their small country house on the banks of the Jordan.

Petra was a breathtaking climax to our visit. A troop of small Arab ponies and their handlers were waiting for us, and we entered the Petra complex through a cleft in the high walled cliffs, so narrow that two people could not travel abreast. Black shadows and shafts of brilliant sunshine alternated, and then suddenly before us, rearing up to a majestic height were the tall columns of Petra's Treasury, lost to the world for six hundred years before being rediscovered in 1812. I was told that more than 30,000 people once lived in Petra, but the whole area has never been explored archeologically. Think how much must be hidden there, what ancient treasures lie beneath the surface. The magic of Petra and most of Jordan is its vivid relationship with Biblical times. The Bedouin tents are still the same as they were thousands of years ago, but now cars and pickups are parked outside them instead of camels. I had resigned myself to the thought that my trekking days were over. Petra was a bonus.

CHAPTER EIGHT

In Waiting

Sometime in 1990 Queen Elizabeth asked me to lunch at Clarence House: Ruth, Lady Fermoy, the exceedingly elegant maternal grandmother of Princess Diana was also there. In her way she was as much a fashion plate as her granddaughter and was a senior Woman of the Bedchamber. When the meal was over Lady Fermoy invited me up to her sitting room. It was all rather mysterious, but she finally got round to the point. To my complete surprise she told me that Queen Elizabeth wanted me as one of her Ladies-in-Waiting, but found it difficult to ask me herself in case I was reluctant. It would have been impossible to say 'No' to her face. My answer, however, was an emphatic and immediate 'Yes'. I had been a widow for nine years and having a job gave me a focus which had been lacking since Denys' death.

I joined a Household which was legendary for its hospitality, conviviality and wit, but underscored by an inexorable sense of duty. It was the unstuffiest of Courts – the animating spirit of all this was, of course, Queen Elizabeth. It was not in her nature to behave as though her privileged position was a crushing burden. By temperament an enjoyer of life, she entered into everything she did with gusto and expected those close to her to do the same. I can only say that I did my best. She turned even the most tedious occasion into a party and from my own experience I fully agree with the anonymous leader writer at *The Times*, who once said of her: 'She lays a foundation stone as though she has discovered a new and delightful way of spending an afternoon'.

She never, however, forgot what she owed to people whose lives were less comfortable, pleasant and interesting than her own. She kept her politics from the public gaze, but no one could say that she leaned towards the Left. Despite this she got on well with many Labour politicians and had a deep concern about social conditions. But I do remember my daughter Annabel having tea with her; and the conversation touching on Tony Blair's then latest wheeze, 'Cool Britannia', prompting Queen Elizabeth to remark wistfully: 'Poor Britannia. She would have hated being Cool'.

When I was recruited there were two Ladies-in-Waiting with titles, who only turned out for the very grandest of occasions and eight Women of the Bedchamber. We 'Women' did fortnightly periods in-'waiting' and accompanied the boss on her official engagements. Our rather elderly entourage was very well briefed on how to behave before we went out to meet the public — as if we didn't know — and the Private Secretary would warn us about any potential trouble spots, like tricky stairs and steps. Fortunately when I was in-'waiting' there were no mishaps, and Queen Elizabeth even coped with the twists and turns of the aircraft carrier 'Ark Royal' without any disasters. We were always supplied with the names of everyone we could possibly meet, and what they were interested in, so that there would be no awkward silences. Our handbags contained the little extra necessities of life to make a Royal visit go like clockwork. I did not know the contents of Her Majesty's handbag, but there was astounded merriment at Clarence House when the satirical magazine *Private Eye* suggested that she never ventured far without an ironed copy of *The Sporting*

Life, a packet of Marks and Spencer chocolate éclairs, a ready mixed gin and Dubonnet in a hip flask and a large number of £50 notes 'just in case'.

The key figures in the Household were Sir Martin Gilliat, the Private Secretary, an ebullient figure who sometimes took on the role of master of the revels; the less ebullient, but wonderfully organised Sir Alastair Aird, the Comptroller, and the Treasurer, Sir Ralph Anstruther, who was a whiz with figures, down to the last decimal point, and who doled out my very modest expenses allowance. Retirement was not an option, except for the young Equerry, always from the Irish Guards, who was seconded to Royal duties for three years.

One of my colleagues, approaching her eightieth birthday, began to drop hints that it was about time for her to go, but before she could breathe another word her employer said: 'Congratulations! You will find that you feel marvellous after you're eighty'. The subject of retirement was never mentioned again. At the time Queen Elizabeth was ninety-eight. It seemed death was the only exit and I sometimes wondered whether my aunt would see me out. She never mentioned dying, only occasionally obliquely referring to someone having 'gone upstairs'.

An example of an intensely loyal courtier staying in post until the end was Martin Gilliat, a very brave man who had been a Colditz prisoner like my brother John. He had been diagnosed with cancer, but although he was seriously ill Queen Elizabeth threw a party in 1993 to celebrate his eightieth birthday, which ended with the usual nostalgic sing song round the piano. Afterwards Martin carried on for more than three months, a shadow of his former sparky self but still forcing himself to work from his flat in St James's Palace. Finally he went into hospital and died three days later. He was much loved and I know Queen Elizabeth deeply mourned the indomitable man who had run both her official and private life for nearly forty years. Shortly afterwards Lady Ruth Fermoy died of inoperable cancer and the two deaths left her bereft.

There were a number of other people in the Household: the Lord Chamberlain, who when I arrived was the Earl of Dalhousie; a Page of Honour, and two Apothecaries — an antique description for the two highly qualified medical consultants who were on call, one for Clarence House and the other for Royal Lodge. There were three secretaries, described as Lady Clerks; one of them worked for the Comptroller, and one for the Ladies-in-Waiting. The third worked in the office of the Press Secretary, Sir John Griffin. Her duties included fielding media calls, and she had a notice pinned on the wall proclaiming: 'We don't leak'. This was in the days when reportage of the Royal Family was running wild and out of control.

The domestic staff was headed by the Housekeeper, and there were also, of course, several footmen, housemaids and chefs. Prominent among this group were the Page of the Backstairs, William Tallon and the Page of the Presence, Reginald Willcock, his close friend. The bouffant haired Mr Tallon was something of a celebrity with the media, which sensed an outré character among an otherwise faceless band of retainers. Like all perfect royal servants he knew his place, but as his work involved close proximity to one of the most photographed women in the world he found it impossible completely to remain in the shadows.

The media dubbed him 'Backstairs Billy' but Queen Elizabeth called him 'William'. I believe there was genuine affection between

Mr Tallon and his employer, and although the upstairs-downstairs rule applied, William and Queen Elizabeth probably met somewhere in the middle. He was her longest serving servant, one of the coterie she regarded as her extended family. Each Christmas she would give him items from a seventy-piece dinner service, and he was close to completing the set when she died. His home, Gate Lodge, at the entrance to Clarence House from the Mall was like a mini Victoria and Albert Museum. It was exquisitely furnished and decorated with gifts from her private collection, and many from long standing friends of my aunt, as well as from William's friends in the ballet and theatre world. He was devastated by her death, which occurred on the fifty-first anniversary of the start of his royal service. With other members of her personal staff, he walked behind her coffin on its journey from the Queen's Chapel at St James's to its lying in state in Westminster Hall, in attendance to the last.

At Clarence House I had a housemaid to look after me, lay my clothes out and pack and unpack for me. She would turn down my bed in the evening and draw the curtains. I could have had breakfast in bed every morning, like some of my more elderly colleagues, but I decided I was not quite old enough for that and anyway couldn't be bothered with the fuss it entailed. This involved a Page leaving the breakfast tray outside the door, retreating out of sight and then a housemaid knocking and carrying it in. I do now, however, allow myself breakfast in bed when I visit Balmoral and Sandringham, my years now meriting this privilege. I knew of course all about curtseying well before I joined the Royal Household. Some people say that they are not curtseying to the individual royal personage, as such, but acknowledging what they represent — the nation. Personally I curtsey to the individual. So curtseying on first seeing Queen Elizabeth in the morning, and on saying goodbye or goodnight was perfectly natural as far as I was concerned.

I knew that my aunt hated stiff formality and that nothing pleased her more than if a Lady-in-Waiting made a mistake, or arrived in the wrong place or at the wrong time. I was able to oblige her early in my service, when she made an early evening visit to the British Library. My first mistake was to wear a hat — hats I later learned were only appropriate for daytime engagements — and was ordered by Martin Gilliat to take it off and lose it. 'No hats in the evening', he said. Then on the way in the car Queen Elizabeth asked me if her hair combs were firmly in place, I lifted my arm to push one in, forgetting I had my handbag on my arm. The bag shot forward and hit her hard on the back of her head. She was angelic enough not to mind. After quite a long time making conversation, I lost her among the crowd, forgetting the very first principle of a Lady-in-Waiting's role — always to keep an eye on the boss. She had simply disappeared and I was told that she had gone. I rushed from the room and down the stairs to an empty hall and a bored looking commissionaire. I thought that this was the end of my 'waiting' career and then I heard a lift descending. Out stepped Queen Elizabeth and Martin, having been to inspect some other department on an upper floor. They hadn't even missed me and I resisted the temptation to say: 'Oh! There you are'. After that salutary experience I never again let her out of my sight.

Official engagements never started before the sun was well and truly up and were conducted at a leisurely pace. Queen Elizabeth liked to give full value, and so they often ran late, which didn't bother her at all, although some members of the Household accompanying her occasionally got twitchy. She had an inherent magic and I have seen even the most die-hard republicans melt when she directed the full beam of her blue eyed charm at them. Her engagements had a sense of the theatre and I remember a royal observer telling me: 'When she steps out of her car it's like curtain up'. She certainly always gave a flawless performance, although I believe it went much deeper than that, because she genuinely liked people of all sorts and conditions. Therefore I have to disagree with the columnist who wrote about her thespian talents on her ninetieth birthday, saying: 'Her Majesty Queen Elizabeth, the Queen Mother is ninety today. No other actress need apply'. But what she did have was the gift of making people believe that they were the only person in the world she wanted to talk to at that given moment. And she had a wonderful sign off line. It went something like this: 'Well, I'd love to stand here talking all day, but I really must get on', as if she had to get home and put the joint in the oven. People were enchanted by this mix of cosiness and glamorous royalty.

It was Thelma Furness, the society beauty of the 1930s, and girl friend of the then Prince of Wales, who once remarked of Queen Elizabeth, who was then Duchess of York: 'If ever I was reduced to living in a bungalow in Bognor, the person I would most like to have living next door to me would be Elizabeth of York'. Quite. Princess Diana also had this gift for scattering star dust, although in a much more overt way. But Queen Elizabeth was compassionate too, although she did not brim over with it before the crowds. She was not one for the binding up of wounds in public. A no-nonsense woman, she did not admit to illness, unless totally unavoidable, and regarded aspirin as a dangerous drug. Her idea for the curing of a bad cold was a bracing walk in a stiff breeze across rugged terrain. It invariably worked! But in her youth and her early years of marriage, she often suffered from a debilitating cough and bad chest.

When I was not trailing round after her coping with the overflow of bouquets and keeping conversation going along VIP line ups, I spent a lot of my time at Clarence House responding to letters. Queen Elizabeth had a huge post, and every letter had to have a response, even if written by some poor person who was mildly deranged. There were quite a few of those, and also from people passionate about various causes, and from children. We tried to be as helpful and kind as we could, but sadly, and very often, there was nothing we could do and the only course of action was to politely tell the writer that we had referred their problem to the appropriate government department. Queen Elizabeth also had an Aladdin's cave of gifts — a big cupboard of china and other bibelots — which could be dipped into, gift wrapped and sent with a letter. Normally the recipients were charities, particularly those local to Windsor; Ballater, near Balmoral, and in Co Durham, where the Bowes family came from. The 9th Earl of Strathmore had married Mary Eleanor Bowes in 1767, the only child and heiress of George Bowes of Streatlam Castle, a rich industrialist. As part of the marriage settlement. he had to take her surname, Bowes, as his own. In her youth, my aunt preferred to be known as Elizabeth Lyon. She did not, however, forsake her north east connection.

What I expected to be my finest hour arrived when one of the

real 'Ladies' went sick and I was commanded to attend a State
Banquet in honour of the King of Malaysia. Queen Elizabeth lent
me a tiara and I felt distinctly grand. The Queen and the state
visitors were led in by David Airlie, the Lord Chamberlain,
carrying his silver wand and walking backwards. The banquet is
the highlight of any state visit. It is a time for an exchange of
compliments and coded messages about foreign policy, spelt out
by host and guest, against a glittering backdrop of gold and silver
gilt plate, candelabra, crystal and massed flowers. The guest list
generally numbers 150, and includes all the members of the Royal
Family who can be mustered; the Archbishop of Canterbury; the
Prime Minister; other members of the Cabinet; representatives of
foreign powers who are friendly to the state visitor; industrialists;
figures from the arts and sometimes a favourite entertainer or
sports person. In the matter of Royal protocol, Queen Elizabeth
always had the Archbishop of Canterbury on her right — at every
single state banquet. The four course meal always has a musical
accompaniment, played by a regimental band, useful for filling
conversational gaps. President Mugabe of Zimbabwe, to mention
just one of the more controversial guests the Queen has had to
entertain over the years, was serenaded with a selection which
included the best of 'Half a Sixpence'; 'I rule the World' and
something called 'Jumping Bean'. The Director of Music gets a
whisky and soda when it is all over.

I wonder if those invited to these occasions realise the amount
of work and planning which goes into them. Damask tablecloths,
some of them more than a century old are brought out to cover
the side serving tables. Every place setting is measured with a
ruler, because no butler worth his salt wants to get to the end of

the table with say, four settings left and nowhere to put them. Late in the afternoon, the Queen, who expects perfection of these occasions, carries out a personal inspection of the tables. Well, there I was amidst all this splendour, sitting next to a man whose firm was supplying a new sewage system to Malaysia. He insisted on passing on every possible detail. It was not a conversation of memorable enjoyment, but of course the food and wine were excellent and to an extent I was able to anaesthetise myself from waste flows and piping in Kuala Lumpur. And it was nice to leave the table at the end and not be faced with the washing up, because below stairs a massive clear up operation was beginning. The 500 crystal glasses; the Minton china; the Sevres or the Meissen-ware; the cutlery were all being washed by hand and stored away, ready for the next time. But, as the Queen says of these occasions and her State visitors: 'We hope to give them a nice time to remember'.

Queen Elizabeth took every opportunity to have lunch *al fresco*. The Clarence House garden has two large plane trees under which tables could be placed. She called this green enclave her *salon verte*. These lunches were jolly occasions, but there is no truth in the story that towards the end of the meal she would order the tables to be moved close to the wall separating the garden from the Mall, so that she could eavesdrop on the conversations of the passers by on the other side, in case they said anything complimentary or otherwise about her. This is a good story, and part of the mythology surrounding her, but moving the tables to such a strategic listening post would have been a physical impossibility because a very large flower bed is in the way. Lunch inside when there were no visitors was held in a corner of the drawing room, and the Lady-in-Waiting would join her. There were always two gentlemen of the Household in attendance to even the numbers. Queen Elizabeth liked to do us well. The chef produced excellent food and the wine was of the best. The meal was always followed by cheeses and then fresh fruit and lastly coffee. She did not at all mind people smoking, saying it reminded her of her husband, her father and her brothers, who all smoked.

A myth, largely media inspired, has grown that she was over fond of drink. It was, I suppose, an almost affectionate canard, and as far as the press was concerned fitted in with the image that she was a good old girl and a sport. All I can say is that her having a drinking habit was simply unimaginable. Her alcohol intake never varied. Before lunch she would have a gin and Dubonnet, with a slice of lemon and a lot of ice. During the meal she might take some wine. In the evening she would have a dry Martini and a glass of champagne with her dinner. There was no excess. In the evenings when we dined alone she liked to watch television as we ate and she thoroughly enjoyed cookery programmes, particularly 'Two Fat Ladies', and comedy shows like 'Dad's Army'. She was amazingly well informed on so many subjects, from gardening, fishing, and racing, to history and European affairs, and even Persian poetry. She was eclectic and would soak up ideas from her wide ranging circle of friends and guests; actors, artists, musicians and poets. She befriended the mystical poet, Edith Sitwell, who, when she was mourning King George VI, sent her a book of poems which comforted her and, she said, made her realise what a selfish thing grief can be.

Another favoured guest was the Poet Laureate, Ted Hughes. One would not have thought that Mr Hughes would have fitted comfortably into what was basically a traditionalist milieu, but

Queen Elizabeth was full of surprises and of catholic taste. He wrote an admiring poem about her on her ninety-fifth birthday comparing her to a six rooted tree. I've never quite been able to work that one out, but it must have been acceptable because in 1998, shortly before he died, he was appointed to the Order of Merit. She would have been pleased when, twelve years after his death he was given a permanent memorial, in Poets' Corner in Westminster Abbey, alongside the great names of British literature, from Chaucer, Shakespeare and Keats, to TS Eliot and WH Auden.

That year, my seventh in 'waiting', did not begin well for my aunt. In January, while visiting the horses in the Sandringham stable yard, she slipped, fell and broke her left hip. I was in the drawing room when she was brought in. She must have been in great pain, but was stoically silent sitting very upright on a chair until the local doctor Ian Campbell arrived. He confirmed that she had broken her hip and an ambulance arrived very quickly. I went with her to the hospital at Kings Lynn, and I remember that she gave me her pearls, brooches and earrings to look after before she was wheeled away for investigation. When I returned to Sandringham there was a lot of discussion about the best course of action. Should she go immediately to London where her own doctors were or be treated by the Norfolk doctors? I thought that the three hour journey to town would be nightmarish in her condition, but it was at length decided that that was the best option for her and I'm sure that she was given a shot of a strong pain killer. The operation took place that evening and later she returned to Clarence House with a new hip to convalesce.

As her ninth decade progressed her family became increasingly worried about the infirmities associated with her great age, and particularly the risk of falling. The Queen sent her a special walking stick, asking her to at least try it, saying that it would make the 'two Margarets'— that is Princess Margaret and myself, Jean, my sister, and not least herself 'very happy and relieved' if she would use it. She did, but under protest. I recall watching her, after one engagement, tossing it with a gesture of contempt into the back of her car. The royal round continued, as did my stints in-'waiting'. They gave a recurring tempo to my life, broken by my much anticipated visits to Scotland. Of all the royal homes Birkhall, on the edge of the Balmoral estate, was the one I most deeply loved. I had been going there since I was five years-old. Before Queen Elizabeth enlarged it, Birkhall was little more than a small eighteenth century dower house. There were few rooms for visitors; the nursery and the sparse accommodation were filled whenever Queen Elizabeth held open house. There was one large room in the tin roofed annexe, where as a child I played with Princess Elizabeth and Princess Margaret.

The burn, the Muick, burbled away at the bottom of the steeply sloping garden and behind rose the fir clad heights of the Coils of Muick. In October the birches turned bright yellow and the rowans scarlet and one could hear the stags roaring their autumnal defiance. At Birkhall lunch was never indoors, whatever the weather, except on Sunday, which had to be observed with some degree of formality, after attending the Kirk. Queen Elizabeth's friends and relations all contributed to the cost of building a charming little wooden cabin beside one of her favourite pools in the river Dee. She called it the 'Old Bull and Bush' after a pub near Hampstead Heath, immortalised in the music hall song 'Down at the Old Bull and Bush' performed by Florrie Forde in the 1920s, when Queen Elizabeth was a girl. She loved the old songs and knew all the words. In another life she might have been a star of the 'Halls'. Dinner at Birkhall could be an uproarious affair. At the end of the meal Queen Elizabeth would start a series of toasts. As well as 'Hooray for...' with glasses held high, there was even more of 'Down with...' with glasses almost disappearing beneath the table. The toasts, combined with the simultaneous chiming of six grandfather clocks, and the community singing — 'Lloyd George knew my Father' was a firm favourite — made for an unforgettable evening. So being in-'waiting' was not all protocol and curtseying: it was, in fact, tremendous fun.

CHAPTER NINE

Afterwards

I greatly enjoyed my eleven years in-'waiting' and the memories are always with me. There are so many happy recollections and the faces of the people I met sometimes pass by in a cavalcade. There were people like Nelson Mandela and the Dalai Lama, who was bursting with smiles, and so overjoyed and full of emotion at meeting Queen Elizabeth that he virtually prostrated himself before her. I seem to remember that he set off his traditional dress with a very smart pair of Bond Street shoes. I like to reflect on the past. It's so much better than watching television.

Clarence House, where I spent so much of my time as a member of the Royal Household, is now the residence of the Prince of Wales and the Duchess of Cornwall when they are in London. He kindly gave a small party for all of us in Queen Elizabeth's Household soon after he took it over — a sort of private view with drinks — and I was delighted to see how beautifully he had restored it. The alterations are designed to reflect the change of occupancy and the colour schemes have been adjusted, but the decoration of the rooms retains the ambience created by Queen Elizabeth and much of her collection of works of art and furniture remain in the places she originally chose for them. However, if only walls could speak!

Birkhall gives the Prince and Duchess a measure of insulation from the pressure of their official lives, but when I was last there

I got quite a jolt when I saw Queen Elizabeth's blue raincoats still hanging in the hall, and this prompted a flood of memories about our windy walks and rain swept picnics. I particularly remember us meeting a group of hikers on their way to the Dubh Loch. Queen Elizabeth had a long conversation with them and up to her death she received an annual Christmas card from 'the hikers of the Dubh Loch'. On another occasion she shared our picnic with some walkers. And what has happened to the 'Old Bull and Bush'?

After Queen Elizabeth died my life changed radically. I was eighty-one, soon to be eighty-two and my social life became minimal, although I have regular stays with the Queen at Balmoral and Sandringham, which, as always, are hugely enjoyable. I know every inch of Balmoral but I am less familiar with Sandringham, which is seductive in an entirely different way. There is not so much as a hill in sight, and Noel Coward was right when he wrote in 'Private Lives', 'very flat, Norfolk'. But you get the huge clouds of the wonderful East Anglian skies and can taste the salt on the wind blowing off the coast which is very close by. I allow myself to be spoilt at Sandringham. I have breakfast in bed, and don't get up before ten in the morning. I read the newspapers and go for long walks: it is all very undemanding. The Queen still rides; sans hard hat, but I don't and fishing and shooting have now become spectator sports for me.

At home the Queen drops in on me sometimes on Sunday after Matins in our little chapel, and we exchange the latest news. I'm still active. No one has taken my driving licence away; woe betide them if they try, and I still do the run to Scotland by car. I do rather a lot of gardening; chugging round the lawns on my tractor-mower and keeping the weeds at bay. My front garden overlooks the Smith's Lawn polo ground and white polo balls have a habit of finding their way into the flower beds.

I go for a walk every day with my West Highland terrier. She is a darling, who has no sense of obedience, never coming when she is called. I had never had a terrier before and have been told that they have a mind set uniquely their own, especially when it comes to chasing rabbits, grey squirrels and pheasants. Living in the Great Park feels like living in proper country, although something of a manicured version. I expected something different when the Queen asked me, with a touch of humour, whether I, a country woman through and through, could tolerate living in 'suburbia'. And, of course, I wouldn't be here but for an accident of birth: that my mother's youngest sister married the Duke of York, later King George VI – and through the kindness of their elder daughter, our Queen.

I have kept the letter that my aunt wrote to my mother after the Duke of York, with his sister, Princess Mary, visited Glamis in the late summer of 1920 and took the first tentative steps towards his courtship of the then Lady Elizabeth Bowes-Lyon. The future Queen Elizabeth, who, at the time had no idea that she was an object of interest to the twenty-four-year-old Duke, told my mother: 'The Duke of York was very pleasant, and has improved immensely in every way. James [Major James Stuart, later Viscount Stuart of Findhorn, and the Duke's Equerry] has worked wonders... I showed the Duke and Princess Mary round the castle; they are really babies and played ridiculous games of hide and seek...but I must say that the Duke was very nice, tho' royalty staying is a nuisance'. The Duke was a rather shy, sensitive young man, plagued by a severe stammer, but he had a streak of pure grit and a not to be beaten attitude to life. It took him almost three years of determined courtship to persuade my aunt to marry him. How fortunate for me that she did!

Most people would say, and I entirely agree with them, that I have been extraordinarily lucky in my life. I had thirty-one years of extremely happy marriage; four children to be proud of; seven grandchildren and two great grandchildren. I have travelled widely and enjoyed the surge of adrenaline in moments of danger. I have been entranced by the dry brown beauty of Africa as well as the blue mistiness of Scotland's Western Isles. I have heard the ugly squabbling laughter of hyenas, as well as the magnificent roaring of Highland stags. I have seen the shimmering beauty of the Taj Mahal and the rawness of a yak herdsman's shelter in the Himalayas.

There are a million things I still want to do and places I long to see, but meanwhile I am a happy and contented person. The children gather round at Christmas, filling my spare beds, with mattresses for my grandchildren. It's chaotic but great fun. My eldest son, Simon, has to my pride and joy become a member of the Royal Company of Archers, of which his Elphinstone grandfather was Captain General. When he was at Harrow he was a Page of Honour to the Queen, having to turn out, dressed in a knee length scarlet coat, a white lace jabot and waistcoat, white breeches, white stockings, black buckled shoes and a small sword. He looked as if he had stepped out of an eighteenth century painting. His most important duty was to hold up, with his three fellow Pages, the Queen's train at the State Opening of Parliament. The long heavy train of the Robe of State needs four pairs of hands, and if it were not carried, the Queen would not be able to move forwards.

Simon was paid £200 a year for this and other ceremonial duties, like the service for the Order of the Garter at Windsor, where the train only needed two pairs of hands. More importantly, as far as he was concerned, was the bonus of getting out of school. He has had his share of adventure. After Harrow we were steering him towards the army or a job in the City, but neither prospect appealed to him and he took off for Africa where his cousin, Robin Plunket, the 8th Baron, had an estate near the Zimbabwe-Mozambique border. It was 1977 and as he made his way out, thousands of expats were heading the other way. I believe it was called the 'chicken run'. He joined the British South African Police. He had, however, no qualms about independence or the inevitability of black rule.

Mugabe was espousing Marxist theory, but not really putting it into practice and so Simon stayed on and later tried his hand at managing a tobacco farm. Denys told everyone that he had become a tobacconist. Then he changed tack and spent four years as a chemical salesman; switching course yet again and going into tourism with Abercrombie & Kent, offering bespoke holidays to wealthy types who wanted to experience the real Africa. But Zimbabwe's internal strife knocked the stuffing out of the holiday trade, and Zimbabwe was lurching towards crisis as Mugabe started his campaign of threats towards white farmers. Things went from bad to worse, and Simon, having been swept up by accident in a Movement for Democratic Change march in Harare, was picked up by the police, badly beaten and charged with incitement to riot. He talked himself out of it and was released, but the experience left him shaken. I was horrified, and told the Queen, who was concerned. And so eventually and reluctantly he returned to Scotland, with his wife Susie, and their two daughters. They were invited to Balmoral by Queen Elizabeth and have now settled in Scotland for good. Simon is now a property developer, based in Perth.

My eldest child, Annabel emigrated to Australia with her first husband and farmed with him in New South Wales. They divorced and she returned home with her baby son. She worked as a secretary in St George's House, Windsor, the residential conference centre close to the castle, in which Prince Philip takes a keen interest, until her remarriage, in 1986, to Charles Cope. They now live in Bideford in Devon, the county in which Denys and I lived so happily for many years.

Victoria, my younger daughter was child orientated from an early age and did a course of Montessori teaching, subsequently working in a Montessori school in London. She married a very distant cousin from New Zealand — sharing a common great grandfather — called Nick Deans who was a sculptor. Soon afterwards Nick had to have a kidney transplant, gallantly donated by his mother. It worked and he was well and healthy for sixteen years, when his kidney failed again. A second implant was unsuccessful and Nick sadly died. Some time afterwards Victoria married John Pryor and together they now run a rather chic delicatessen at Cley on the north Norfolk coast.

Michael, my youngest son, like Simon went to Harrow, and like me, and his Elphinstone grandfather, has itchy feet, travelling extensively. He read law at West of England University in Bristol, but his gardening genes, probably inherited from my mother, took over, and quite simply he is very happy earning his living by looking after people's gardens. He too lives in Norfolk.

Among my grandchildren I have an artist, a writer and a practitioner of Japanese medical science. Life is never dull, but when they were growing up I kept on pushing the idea that they should acquire some practical skills, so as to have something to fall back on, like plumbing. Plumbers, I protested, were always in demand.

Queen Elizabeth would sometimes remark that my attendance at church was tardy — she never missed — but I actually have a firm faith, and am convinced that I shall be reunited with Denys. My belief in the afterlife has been confirmed by the experience of my daughter Victoria who, after Nick died, felt compelled one day to visit the woman doctor who treated him in hospital. She told my daughter about an extraordinary dream she had had the night before, in which a youthful and fit Nick appeared, telling her: 'Look, I know that Vic is taking it very badly, but you must tell her that all is well with me, and not to be sad'. Perhaps it is my Strathmore heritage but that story confirmed my own belief in something better 'upstairs' as Queen Elizabeth described the exit lounge of mortality.

I have now been to the funerals of all my brothers and sisters. It makes me feel rather like a species of dinosaur left behind by evolution. There are no close Elphinstone family members of my generation left to ask: 'Do you remember?' or 'What happened then?' On the other hand there is a great sense of relief that I can be just myself; get up when I like; go to bed when I like and have my meals when I like. I no longer really mind what other people think, and so there is much to be said for antediluvian freedom.

My eldest brother John, the 17th Lord Elphinstone, died in 1975. My younger brother, Andrew, predeceased him that same year, and so Andrew's son James became the 18th Lord Elphinstone. Sadly he died young and the present Lord Elphinstone is his eldest son Alexander. My eldest sister, Elizabeth, died in 1980, on the very day that the 'Old Bull and Bush' was presented to Queen Elizabeth as a birthday present. It was an awful shock. My sister had been a bridesmaid at my aunt's wedding to the Duke of York, and they had always been close. Only eleven years separated them, and they were more like sisters than aunt and niece. However, the inauguration of the 'Old Bull and Bush' had to go ahead, as Queen Elizabeth did not want to disappoint the many friends who had travelled to Scotland for the occasion. My sister Elizabeth's death cast a shadow over an otherwise lovely day, but she was well remembered during the long and lively lunch presided over by her aunt. Elizabeth was fourteen years older than me; very kind and loving. She was keen on ornithology and we would spend long, cold hours, scanning the beaches of Aberlady, trying to identify ducks and waders. She was also keen on God and when she was in an evangelising mood would lure me into her bedroom to pray. She was dismayed that I did not take this seriously enough. I found it positively embarrassing to kneel down, in cold blood so to speak, and try to talk to my maker.

Elizabeth never married and, being very holy in the sweetest way, helped the Christian author Amy Buller, whose writings had much impressed Queen Elizabeth, to set up the King George VI and Queen Elizabeth Foundation of St Catherine in Cumberland Lodge, not far from where I live in Windsor Great Park. The Foundation now runs residential courses for students who go there to examine, in the context of Christian philosophy, the fundamental assumptions underlying political, economic, and scientific activities.

My other sister Jean died in 1999, a few weeks after her husband Major John Wills. She suffered a heart attack during a lunch party given by Queen Elizabeth at Clarence House after the memorial service for Lord Dalhousie, her Lord Chamberlain. Queen Elizabeth calmly led her guests from the room, while Jean was given medical attention. She died later the same day in hospital. Jean put great store on royalty, and it became a rather bad family joke that it suited her beautifully to die (almost) in a grand royal residence. Jean was more lively than Elizabeth. She lived quite close to me and we saw a lot of each other. I well remember the day she telephoned me in a panic. Her cook had succumbed to a virus and she was due to give a dinner party that night with the sometimes demanding Princess Margaret as the guest of honour. I immediately volunteered my services as cook, so as to free the hostess to be gracious, cool and entertaining. The first course was some sort of cold dish, followed by poussin, neither of which presented any problems. I derived some wry amusement from observing the guests through the serving hatch, as I knew most of them and wondered whether they had guessed the true identity of the Mrs Bridges in the kitchen.

Jean wanted a cheese soufflé as the savoury, and this threw me. The timing for a soufflé is critical, as it is liable to collapse. My soufflé refused to perform, resting lifeless in the unpredictable Aga, as the empty chicken plates returned and the guests began to wonder when the next course was coming. I fell to my knees in front of the oven and began to pray to whichever saint prevents culinary disasters. Miraculously the soufflé began to rise and I was able to deliver perfection. Jean had hired an occasional butler for the evening, and we became friends in adversity. Shortly afterwards I was invited to dinner by some neighbours, only to find my new friend the butler in attendance. He was deeply shocked that the cook should presume to attempt admittance to the kitchen through the front door!

Life has been packed with adventures, and over the years I have attempted to chronicle my own experiences on a typewriter which is almost an antique. The pages have grown into a pile and look rather yellow. I like to think that my story punctuates social history as I have lived it. I have certainly loved every minute of it so far, but I am convinced that the last great adventure is still to come.

* * *

As a postscript to the above, I recently went to see the film, 'The King's Speech'. I found it immensely moving and felt that it was as reasonably accurate as was possible. Indeed tears flowed at various moments.